John Williams

Historical Notes on Wallington

John Williams

Historical Notes on Wallington

ISBN/EAN: 9783337042424

Printed in Europe, USA, Canada, Australia, Japan

Cover: Foto ©ninafisch / pixelio.de

More available books at **www.hansebooks.com**

HISTORICAL
NOTES ON WALLINGTON:

OF WHICH THE SUBSTANCE WAS GIVEN IN

A LECTURE AT WALLINGTON SCHOOLS IN 1870; WITH

ADDITIONS TO THE PRESENT TIME.

BY

THE REV. JOHN WILLIAMS, M.A.,

VICAR OF HOLY TRINITY, WALLINGTON,

SURREY.

WITH ILLUSTRATIONS.

———

" Ex fumo dare lucem."—
Hor. de Arte Poet.

———

LONDON:

W. MACKINTOSH, 24, PATERNOSTER ROW.

WALLINGTON:

W. PILE, 5, DANBURY TERRACE.

PREFACE.

THE origin of this compilation appears on the Title-page. Indulging a natural curiosity as to the past in the history of his Parish, the compiler collected notes, to divert some of his less busy hours. The County Histories supplied abundant material. Then arose the idea of a Lecture on the subject, in the Parish Schoolroom, at our Winter Evening Entertainments. Therefore to the enumeration of individuals and families, comments were added to elucidate the cotemporary events, in which some of those connected with Wallington played a part. What then might appear to some only digressions, had for their object the supplying of that necessary information which the generality have no opportunity to acquire; while it was hoped that thus would be enlarged the sympathy which each should feel as a unit of the great Commonwealth. The Lecture, however, furnished entertainment for one evening. But when "My Garden," with its charming illustrations, had seen the light, there arose a desire to know more of Wallington. And so the Lecture recurred to our enterprising Bookseller.

The original material has been re-written for his use, retaining its first characters, only more fully given. Many kind friends, whose names might occupy some pages, have aided ; and a visit to the British Museum has helped to fill some gaps in the story.

The pressure of Parish work under somewhat exceptional circumstances will, it is hoped, be some excuse for deficiencies.

Such as it is, the Parishioners of Holy Trinity, Wallington, will accept it, as it was always intended for THEIR "*entertainment*," by their sincere friend and Pastor,

J. WILLIAMS.

March, 1873.

HISTORICAL NOTES.

"HISTORICAL NOTES ON WALLINGTON" should not allow any great indulgence of fancy. They should not allow us to be tempted to plunge into mother earth, and seek geological treasures, however sure that our search will be rewarded. And so we pass by palæontology, zoology, conchology, &c. Nor should we feel at liberty to indulge in reveries as to the *Stone* age of the world's inhabitants—before the days of Tubal-cain and artificers in brass and iron, (Gen. iv. 22)?— though there lacks not the temptation in the beautiful little Celt hatchet which our friend Mr. Jas. West (now departed) found only the other day ; and then again a similar implement which Mr. Cressingham found in the field adjoining "My Garden," and which Mr. Smee has figured in his book (p. 2). Nor should the thought of Dr. Strong's "*bronze* Celts recently excavated at Beddington" lead us astray. For we must beware of exciting any envious feelings in the breasts of our Welsh cousins with their Celtic Pedigree, and its Historical Notes—"about this time Noah was born"—not quite at the top of the Tree.

But what can we do when a friend begs us to notice the "Hut-circles"—traces of the dwellings of our forefathers long, long ago? These are "peculiar circular hollows, like "inverted cones having sloping sides narrowing to a point

B

" at the extremity, and upon these, most probably, ledges of
" earth were formed to be used as seats or sleeping places.
" The pit was covered over by long poles laid sloping from
" the sides and meeting in a point overhead in the centre,
" and coated with rough boughs and turf to exclude the
" wet and cold, as the hop-pickers in Kent might shelter
" themselves in their season, or the charcoal-burners among
" the Surrey and Sussex hills.   Traces of Hut-circles are to
" be seen in the fields S.E. of Woodcote ; more especially
" very distinct traces of one to the N.E. of Wallington
" Manor House, just to the left of the footpath by the Paper
" Mill from Wallington Bridge to the Beddington and
" Croydon Road " (the very spot where Mr. Cressingham's
Celt should have been found), " there appears to have been
" a rampart—with the peculiarity of having been square on
" plan—around this ; and the southern slope of the bank,
" which is crossed by the footpath, is very distinct.

"There appears to have been another to the S.W. of
" Wallington Church, close to the roadway to the station,
" but a rough unshapely hollow in the lavender field, only,
" remains.   The form of this has been much altered."

So our many temptations are apparent. Yet we must
forbear.   For we shall have to draw somewhat on the
forbearance of our friends when we treat of the site of the
ancient " Noviomagus " supposed to be in our Parish.   But
we will be cautious even with the Roman historians, lest
some Wallington Edie Ochiltree rise up and cry, as the
original did to Mr. Oldbuck, " Prætorium here, prætorium
there—I mind the biggin o't."

" Historical Notes " in reference to any part of England
cannot commence before the year B.C. 55, when the ambition

of the Roman general, Julius Cæsar, led him to invade Britain. After having been somewhat roughly handled, he returned to Gaul; and, in the following year, with a force of 32,000 men, he landed somewhere near Sandwich. He first came in contact with the British forces at or near the spot where the city of Canterbury now stands. Thence he penetrated through Kent and a part of Surrey, not improbably passing through our parish, and crossed the Thames at Coway Stakes, near Chertsey. Roman discipline soon prevailed over a disunited people; but Cæsar was glad to accede to overtures for peace, and to return to Gaul It was not till about A.D. 84 that the Roman dominion in Britain was consolidated under Agricola, and by that time the Island had attracted attention from the more civilized parts of the world. The Romans had introduced their manners and laws; a strong body of troops maintained the occupation of the country; and, between the different districts, solidly-made roads afforded proper means of communication. Britain formed an essential part of the Roman Empire.

It is supposed that at this period the town of Nœomagus (or Noviomagus) occupied the southern portion of our parish. A town of this name is mentioned by the geographer Ptolemy; and a similar name "Noviomagus" occurs in the Antonine Itinerary. Ptolemy lived at Alexandria, in Egypt, about 130 A.D. To him is referred the Ptolemaic system of astronomy which made the earth the centre of our universe—a system, which though false in fact and absurd in theory, was maintained for 1400 years; till Nicholas Copernicus, of Thorn, in Polish Prussia, discovered the system which goes by his name, and of which the truth

B 2

has been fully established by Kepler, Galileo and Newton. The industry of Ptolemy collected much valuable information, though some of his statements are incorrect. What is interesting to us we find stated in his geography of Britain: "again to the south of the Atrebatii and Cantii lie the Regni and the city of Nœomagus. Long. 19° 45″ Lat. 53° 25″." (See Appendix A.) Doubtless Ptolemy had never visited Britain, and obtained his information from others. So, perhaps, the only reliable fact is that this town was among the people called Regni, who occupied the present counties of Surrey and Sussex. Chichester was called Regnum by the Romans.

The Antonine Itinerary seems to have been compiled about A.D. 200, and supplies us with such information about the towns on certain routes, and the distances between them, as the commanders of Roman armies issued for the guidance of their troops on a line of march.

Thus in Iter. II of the Antonine Itinerary the route from London to Richborough (then one of the chief Roman stations) is thus laid down:—

Noviomago	x M.P. (Roman miles) presumed sites.	
Vagniacis	xviii „	—	„
Durobrivis	ix „	—	Rochester.
Durolevo	xvi „	—	„
Duroverno	xii „	—	Canterbury.
ad portum Ritupis x „	—	Richborough.

ITER. III.		Roman miles.
a Londinio ad Portum Dubris	lxvi	from London to Dover.
Durobrivis	xxvii	Rochester.
Duroverno	xxv	Canterbury.
ad portum Dubris	xiv	Dover.

ITER. IV.		Roman miles.
a Londinio ad portum Lemanis	lxviii	from London to Lymne.
Durobrivis	xxvii	Rochester.
Duroverno	xxv	Canterbury.
ad portum Lemanis	xvi	Lymne.

Then there is the Itinerary of Richard of Cirencester in the 14th century, who says he compiled from ancient documents; of a similar character to those from which the Antonine Itinerary was compiled. An interesting publication took place A.D. 1598 of Tables of a corresponding style, supposed to be of the time of Theodosius the Great, A.D. 379, and found among the MSS. in the library of Conrade Peutinger—hence called the Peutinger Tables.

Iter I, of Richard of Cirencester, is, from Rhutupis, by the viâ Guethelinga (Watling Street), to—

Cantiopoli quœ est Duroverno	-	-	x M.P.
Durosevo (Durolevo)	-	-	-	-	xii „
Duroprovis (Durobrivis) -	-	-	-	xxiv „
Deinde (thence) Londinium	-	-	xxvii „

ITER. XV. CANTIOPOLI.

Durolevo	-	xviii M.P.		Noviomago	-	xviii M.P.
Mado	- -	xii „		Londinio	-	xv „
Vagnaca	-	xviii „			

ITER. XVII.

ab Anderida	-	Pevensey.
Silva Anderida	-	The great wood of Anderida, now "Weald" of Sussex.
Noviomago	- -	„
Londinio	xv	„

What can we gather from these Tables was the site of Noviomagus? or Nœomagus? Comparing them with each other we learn a little of their relative value.

In the Antonine Iter II, we find the distance given from London to Durobrivis (*Rochester*) to be 37 Roman miles passing by Noviomagus. But in Iter. III and IV it is 27 only, and in the Iter. I of Richard of Cirencester, the same distance (27 Roman miles) is given; and in this Iter, the distance from Duroverno (*Canterbury*) to London is 63 miles by Durobrivis along the old Watling Street road, on which

Noviomagus is not mentioned. But in Iter XV, which passes by Noviomagus, the distance from Canterbury to London is made 81 miles, and on this route Durobrivis is not mentioned. So here we have two Itineraries making *Noviomagus* appear *out of the direct route.* In the distance from London to Rochester it is 10 Roman miles out of the direct route, and in that to Canterbury, 13 miles. The actual distances from London to Rochester—30 miles—and to Canterbury—56 miles English (statute measure)—would make the Itineraries a good deal out in their reckonings for the direct routes. Again we observe a difference as to the distance of Noviomagus from London : in the Antonine Itinerary it is X, M.P., but in that of Rd. of Cirencester it is XV, M.P.; very different routes from the Antonine.

Ought we not to conclude that the distances given are only approximate? not exact? and that we can wholly depend on neither, when both are proved to be wrong?— *proved,* because we can certainly identify some sites, such as Rochester and Canterbury—and correct the distances given—but how shall we deal with the uncertain; as Noviomagus ?

We will endeavour to view the question in another light. We will see if the generally acknowledged traces of Roman Roads in our neighbourhood will help our enquiry. · Traces are found of a Roman Road first from Chichester—which in part of its course is called *Stane Street.* It passes by Billinghurst, in Sussex; then by *Anstiebury Camp,* near Dorking; then by the back of Woodcote Warren, in Epsom, and leaving Burgh or Barrow, in Banstead, on the right, goes to Streatham. This road must have passed through our parish.

We will take *another* road from Portus Adurni (SHOREHAM) traced in the "Gentleman's Magazine" for July, 1781, across Sussex into Surrey. A *third* from the Portus Anderida (PEVENSEY), according to Mr. Leman, coincided with the preceding after passing into Surrey; and these two fall into a *fourth* road from Portus Novus (NEWHAVEN), passing by Lindfield and E. Grinstead, in Sussex, New Chapel, in the parish of Godstone; over Tilbuster Hill; through Blechingley, Chaldon and Coulsdon to Streatham. It was directly on this route that the late Mr. Jas. West saw Roman bricks found; and " a *paved causeway*," when some labourers were grubbing a coppice on Mrs. Gee's land; by the road passing from Farthing Down and Russell Hill to Bandon Hill—Roman *buildings* as well as a *road* thus indicated.

And yet another *fifth* road we must allude to as mentioned in Camden (quoting from Higden of Chester), "a consular way of the Romans which formerly went from Dover through the middle of Kent." Camden would make Maidstone the site of Vagnaca, so called from the river Vaga (Medway), called in the Peutegerian Tables *Madus*. And still further it is suggested by Bray, that there was a line of road (Roman) through Newdi*gate*, Rey*gate*, *Gate*ton, Chipstead, and Leaden Cross.

Surely all these roads pointing to and converging in or about the Southern part of our Parish would prove it to be an important position in the times of the Romans in England.

Confirmation of this idea may be found in the numerous relics brought to light from time to time. In Salmon's History of Surrey (A.D. 1736) mention is made of " Barrows "or small mounds (on the rising ground above Barrow-

" Hedges), called in that day *Gally Hills*, which means
" *Devil's mounds*. About Woodcote were considerable traces
" of buildings; axes and spear-heads had been continually
" found in the fields; and many old wells," (which *remain
to this day of* 1872). The present proprietor of Woodcote
mentions a peculiar large ivory ball found there, but which
was unfortunately stolen; and he points to a mound in the
ground near the House, which should be opened.

In the neighbourhood of our Church, Roman relics have
been frequently found in the shape of *coins*. In the little
Museum at Beddington School, which Rev. Jas. Hamilton
instituted, are some coins presented by Mr. Lee, of Wallington. Mr. Robt. Matthews has kindly lent us for inspection
some coins which he has dug up from time to time: his, as
well as Mr. Lee's, all found in the immediate neighbourhood
of our Church.

Then we have the Roman Villa, be it large or small,
discovered in February, 1871, on the Farm occupied by the
Croydon Local Board of Health—between Beddington Lane
and Hackbridge Station. The discovery was communicated
to the Society of Antiquaries, and papers read by
J. Addy, Esq., Stud. C.E., and E. P. Loftus Brock, Esq.
A list of the coins appears in Appendix B, with the
description of the Roman Villa.

The site of this Villa would be very nearly in the direct
line from Woodcote to Streatham. The dates of coins may
be presumed to give a fair idea of the date of building—
not accurately, but nearly so. And the sum total of the
evidence from the coins would give a Roman occupation of
the locality through, at least, one hundred and fifty years,
dating, as they do, from A.D. 258 to A.D. 375. One of

Commodus, found near the Villa, will date at A.D. 176.
But of the *British City* we should scarcely expect to find
traces if we take Cæsar's description as correct (lib. v. c. 21) :
"The Britons call it a Town, when they have strengthened
"a wood by a rampart and ditch ; where they may be
"protected from an incursion of enemies."

But we may suppose the neighbourhood was a favourite
resort in very early times, if we may judge from the hoard
of Bronze implements now in the possession of Dr. Strong,
of Croydon, found in preparing the foundations of a house
nearly opposite the Beddington Schools—(J. W. Flower,
Esq., F.G.S.)—"probably part of the stock-in-trade of some
manufacturer of such implements."

At any rate the locality, on the edge of the "Surrey hills,"
with an extensive prospect of the valley of the Thames,
above London as far as Windsor; and with rich meadows
on the banks of the Wandle beneath, must have had an
attraction. Nor is it unlikely that the river received its
distinctive name from some *Vandal* (WEND) soldier of for-
tune coming to England with the Roman troops sent by
Probus (A.D. 276) ; who, having settled down hereabouts,
if he did not occupy the Roman Villa at Beddington, gave
his name to the river, Pope's "blue transparent Vandalis,"
and the town at its mouth, *Wandsworth—Wandlesorde* of
Domesday Book. (Bartlett's History of Wimbledon.)
Wendel's choice was good, and after-ages still hovered
around the spot in fixing site of the Manor House.

However, the Anglo-Saxons showed their taste in fixing
their residences hereabouts ; amid the varied scenery of
hill and dale, beautiful woods and water, arable and pasture
land. We have an Anglo-Saxon Cemetery at Farthing

Down, in Coulsdon, explored by Mr. Flower; an Anglo-
Saxon Cemetery in the same field with the Roman Villa,
which Mr. Addy and Mr. Smee explored, and in the Villa
itself a Saxon penny was found. All these discoveries are
chronicled in the Surrey Archæological Society's sixth
volume. And in the publications of the British Archæological Association, Mr. Brock relates, that in digging
foundations for the houses, about three feet below the
surface, there were found, alongside the "Manor Road,"
six graves of the Anglo-Saxon period. When the foundations were dug for the house where Mrs. West now resides,
sixty years ago, a skeleton in a sitting posture was found;
and at frequent intervals broken weapons and armour have
been found in the land to the E. of Manor Road—precious
relics gone! none can tell whither.

A curious history all these relics might teach us. And
we may fairly gather from the notes above, as Manning
argues: "that Woodcote was a Camp or Town, there can
be no doubt—perhaps the former—and Wallington the
Town below it. Romans at least did not place cities on an
eminence, but camps; and towns below." And (we add)
the patrician Villa was thus placed on the banks of the
Wandle, the most favourable spot for the garden and farm
adjoining. "A noble house, which stands in a choice air,"
so Walton describes *Dauntsey*, where George Herbert stayed
long—it being in fact a marshy place by the side of a river,
as its name betokens.

Throughout the country Roman Villas were frequent,
along the great roads especially. Caracalla (A.D. 211)
imparted the rights and privileges of the Roman citizen to
all the provinces of the Empire, and thus the Briton enjoyed

his patrimony without fear of spoliation or oppression. But while there was peace under the Roman sway, new enemies were rising up. The Scandinavian and Saxon Pirates began to ravage the S. and S.E. coasts—some, indeed, had already settled there. To repress these marauders a Roman officer was appointed, with the title "Count of the Saxon shore." To this office Carausius (by birth either a Belgian or Briton), was appointed, with the command of a strong fleet, the head-quarters of which were in the British Channel. He was a bold and skilful commander, but made himself feared and suspected by the Roman Emperors, who sent orders to put him to death. In answer, he gathered around him the sailors and soldiers who had enriched themselves under his command, and by them he was proclaimed Emperor, which title was conceded to him at Rome, with the government of Britain and the adjoining coasts of Gaul. Under his reign Britain figured as a great naval power. He struck numerous medals and coins, with inscriptions and devices, which show the pomp and state he assumed in his island empire. He was murdered A.D. 297, at York, by *Allectus*. a Briton, who succeeded to his insular empire, and reigned about three years, when he was defeated and slain by an officer of Constantius Chlorus, to whom Britain fell in succession, on the resignation of Diocletian and Maximian. Constantine Chlorus died at York, A.D. 306, and was succeeded by his son Constantine, afterwards called the Great (whose mother, Helena, was a British lady). There are few things in history more romantic than the account of the fortunes of Helena. The daughter of a British inn-keeper, who seems to have had his house on one of the great Roman roads in Britain, and acting in her father's establishment as hostelress (*stabularia*), won the affections of a great Roman general, who, not ashamed of his choice, united himself to her in honourable marriage. And so the British maiden, without wealth for a dowry, came to be the mother of the Emperor of the world—yet, her greatest honour that she, with her son, were not ashamed to profess themselves Christians.

The Roman power, however, was waning, and the removal of the capital of the empire from Rome to Constantinople had its effects on the remote provinces of Britain. Following an example which had become prevalent throughout the empire, and first set in Britain by Carausius, several officers set up for themselves as independent sovereigns. Historians of that period describe Britain as especially fertile in that class of productions. One of the most noted who raised the standard of revolt in this country was Maximus (A.D. 382)—probably connected with the Imperial family of Constantine. He was associated with *Gratian*, and on his death, he succeeded to the Empire of the West.

A.D. 420 the Romans retired from Britain, and the country soon fell an easy prey into the hands of Saxon and Danish marauders. At first they seem to have carried only ruin wherever they passed. But gradually they settled down, and generally selected stations that had previously been occupied by the Romans. Thus the Roman "Regnum" was occupied under the name of *Cissan-ceaster*, the *castrum* (Roman camp) of *Cissa* (the *Saxon*)—*Chichester*. That our neighbourhood was extensively occupied by them, we have seen already. What was the fate of the ancient Town hereabouts is left to conjecture. But amid the contests of Briton, and Saxon, and Dane; frequent in this neighbourhood—at Wimbledon notably—it is not likely that a *town* at Wallington would be spared. Still the memory of such a place survives in the name given by the Saxons to the Hundred division of the County—Waletone; for what is this but *Vallum-tone*—retaining the old Roman mark— "Rampart, or camp," with the Saxon addition, "tone" or town? We have in our own neighbourhood two *Waltons*, besides our own, both of which have evident traces of camps. Many instances might be adduced where the Saxons, changing the name of a place, still preserved, in its changed name, tokens of its previous Roman occupation.

When the Saxons had settled down in Britain, they gradually introduced the customs and laws which had been popular with them in their North-German homes. Hence the division of the kingdom into Counties, sub-divided into Hundreds, which again were sub-divided into Tithings, or Parishes, afterwards. The place which would give the name to the Hundred would, on some account or other, be the most notable place in the neighbourhood. Such was the Town in our Parish—the most noteworthy of the Waletons. Such was the *Thorn tree on the Hill-top*—where the Saxon Councils assembled on grand occasions—and which gave the name to *Copthorne* Hundred.

With A.D. 1066 came the Norman invasion. Harold, and his brothers, and nearly all the nobility of the South, perished at the battle of Hastings. The Norman host spread over Surrey; everything valuable was plundered by the soldiers; what they could not carry away was committed to the flames; and so our Town had its misfortunes among the rest! But in due time the Norman rule was established, and the Conqueror desired to have a record of the obligations under which his subjects held their land. So Domesday Book was compiled. Its origin may be thus stated : The military constitution of the Saxons having been abolished, the nation was without an army, and an invasion of the Danes being apprehended, a Great Council was held at Sarum, in which it was resolved to establish feudal tenures. Commissioners were appointed to obtain information from juries of the different Hundreds, in every county, of the quantity of land in all manors ; the names of the superior lords and sub-tenants; and the amount of *Danegeld* paid in the reign of Edward the Confessor. The returns were transmitted to the Exchequer at Winchester, and were there arranged in the *Domesday Book.* On the opposite page there is a fair fac-simile of so much as concerns us in the Domesday Book, except that there are some red lines across the name *Waleton,* and the word Rex has a little red.

The extract given presents the Latin words in their contracted form ; here the words are given in full, and what is supplied is printed in italics, as given in Manning :

" Rex ten*et* in dom*i*nio Waletone. *Tempore* Reg*is* Ed*wardi* et m*odo* se def*endebat* pro xi hid*is.* Ter*r*a *est* xi carrucata*rum.* In dom*i*nio *est* una carruc*ata* et xv vill*ani* et xiii Bord*arii* cum x car*r*uc*atis.* Ibi iii servi, et ii molini de xxx solid*is,* et viii acr*œ* prati. Silv*á* quæ *est* in Chent.

" Ricard*us* de Tonebrige ten*et* de hoc m*a*ner*io* unam virgat*am* cum silva, unde abstulit rusticu*m* qui ibi manebat. N*u*nc reddit vicecomiti x sol*idos* per annum. Tot*um* manerium *Tempore* Reg*is* Ed*wardi* valeb*at* xv libr*as.* Modo x libr*as.*"

Here, then, we are struggling into clearer light with our

R ge ten' in dnio Waletone. T.R.E. 7 in se defd
p. xi. hid. Tpa e. xi. car'. In dnio e una car'. 7 xcv.
uitti 7 xxii. bord' cu x. car'. Ibi. iii. serui. 7 ii. molini
de xx. solid. 7 viii. de pa. Silua que e in chent:
Ricard' de Tonebrige ten' de hoc m una uirgata
in silua. unde abstulit pastu qui ibi manebat. Nc
reddit uicecomiti. x. sol. p annu.
Totu m T.R.E. ualb. xv. lib. Modo. xc. lib.

" Historical Notes," and we can identify ourselves in the
Domesday Book—which retains the Saxon name of the
Hundred. We will give a free—very free—translation of
the above. We read: "The king holds Wallington in
demesne, for his own profit." (The crown held altogether
1422 manors—14 in Surrey—which had chiefly belonged
to the Saxon kings, Edward the Confessor, Harold, etc.)
" In the time of Edward the Confessor and now, it has been
rated for eleven hides." (That would be as much as eleven
ploughs could cultivate in the year; the measurement
varied, probably according to the quality of the soil—some
make a hide to be 100 acres, others 120.) " The arable land
is eleven carrucates." (A carrucate was same quantity as
a hide.) " In demesne for his own use, the lord retains one
carrucate. There are with ten carrucates, xv villagers;"
(who are bound to remain with their children and effects,
ready to be employed in any servile work for the lord);
"there also xiv Bordarii" (of less servile condition than the
Villani, supplying the lord with poultry, eggs, &c.; grind-
for him, threshing, drawing wood); "there also three
slaves" (of lower. condition than the Villani, wholly
dependent on the lord's will); "there are two mills worth
30s., and viii acres " (an acre was 120 square perches) "of
meadow, besides a wood in Kent," not included in the eleven
hides above.

" Richard de Tonbridge holds of this manor one virgate
(a quarter of a hide) with a wood, whence he carried off
the villagers who used to dwell there. He now pays for
these lands 10s. per ann. The whole manor in the time of
King Edward was valued at xv pounds, now at x pounds."

The shilling mentioned above was only money of account.

There was no such *coin* then. The Saxon shilling consisted of fivepence; the Domesday, of twelvepence. The libra or pound in money was made of 12 ora, valued at 20d. to the ora. Here we have something like our Duodecimal system.

And now, not to incur the charge of being unneighbourly, as we shared with Beddington the glories of Celtic, British, Roman, and Saxon antiquity, we will share the glory of Domesday.

But our publisher cannot afford more than one fac-simile, and it is likely most of our readers will not care for the Latin version, so we will give them in plain English what is said in Domesday about Beddington. We will premise, however, that though we can claim no Roman origin for the name, we can fairly assume that the name is of Saxon origin; and *Beddintone* of Domesday may mean the Town or dwelling-place of the Bede family, as Beddingfield, in Suffolk, and Beddingham, in Norfolk (so Lower); and as Mr. Flower reminds us, a name illustrious in English History as having been borne by the "Venerable Bede." There were two manors.

1. "Robert de Wateville holds of Richard [de Tonbridge] Beddintone, which Azor held of King Edward. It was then assessed for xxv hides; now at iii hides. The arable land consists of vi carrucates. One carrucate is in demesne, and there are xvi villagers and xiv cottars with v carrucates. There is a *Church*, and five slaves, and two mills valued at forty shillings, and 24 acres of meadow. The wood is sufficient for five pigs. Fifteen houses in London belong to this manor, paying 12 shillings and 4 pence. In the time of King Edward it was valued at £10, and the same at present, but when received it was reckoned at £6 only."

2. " Milo Crispin holds Beddintone, and William the son of Turold holds it of him. Ulf held it of King Edward, and it was then assessed at 25 hides, now at three only. There are 6 carrucates of land arable, one is in demesne; and 13 villagers and 13 cottagers have 6 carrucates. There is one bondsman, and two mills valued at 35s., and 20 acres of meadow. The wood suffices for five pigs.

"In the time of King Edward, the manor was valued at £10; afterwards at £6, and now at £9 10s. Twenty-one houses (13 in London and 8 in Southwark) belonging to this manor, which pay 12s., have been detached, and are held by Earl Roger" [de Montgomery].

We gather a good deal from the above as to the state of cultivation and population of the locality. But still it must be remembered a good deal is left out in Domesday, though what is there, may be depended on. Its testimony is unimpeachable in our Law Courts.

The next authentic record of Wallington we shall take, will be the " *Testa de Nevill,*" compiled A.D. 1327, at latest. There, it is stated that Henry II. (between 1154—1189) granted part of the Royal Manor of Wallington to *Maurice de Creon.* This name occurs in connection with the neighbouring parishes of Norbiton, Ham, and Ewell. When the King's daughter, Matilda, was married, he was assessed in £15 " *aid.*" He was one of three Barons, chosen with three Bishops, for arbiters in the league Henry made with Lewis, of France, to go to the Holy Land. His son Guy succeeded him, 34th of Henry II., paying a fine of £134 13s. 4d. for livery of the lands which his father held, and afterwards he went with Richard I. to the Holy Land, A.D. 1188—the third Crusade.

c

Doubtless the dwellers in the neighbourhood received an
additional impulse in favour of the Crusades from the fact
that a daughter of Geoffrey de Manneville, of Carshalton,
had married a son of Eustace, of Boulogne, who was father
(by his second wife, Ida, of Loraine), of Godfrey, the first
Christian king of Jerusalem, A.D. 1099.

The Crusades may be said to have originated with an
English lady, Helena, the mother of Constantine the Great,
attempting to fix the spot where her "newly adopted faith
had found its cradle and reared its stage." From that time
forward, pilgrimages to the Holy City became a practice
among Christians ; and, as Christianity became corrupt,
such pilgrimages were regarded as deeds of exalted piety,
certain of receiving a glorious recompense. Then the disciples of the false Prophet obtained possession of the Holy
Land, and under Mohammedan rule, the Christian pilgrim
suffered dreadful treatment and exactions. Pope Sylvester
II. originated the idea of a Crusade, towards the close of
the tenth century. But the work of arming Christendom
under the banner of the Cross, against the Infidel, was
reserved for Peter the Hermit—*eleventh* century. In
the first Crusade, A.D. 1096, the English, as a nation,
can scarcely be said to have concerned themselves; though
Robert, Duke of Normandy, the eldest son of William I.
bore a distinguished part in it. It was in the third Crusade
that England appeared most illustrious, in the person of
Richard I ; though perhaps never did the armies of Europe
leave its shores, without being accompanied by British
soldiers and sustained by British wealth. "England,"
Fuller remarks, " was in that age the Pope's packhorse, and
seldom rested in the stable when there was any work to be

done." Again, in the ninth and last Crusade, A.D. 1270, our Edward I. set forth, and with him our Carshalton neighbour, William de Fielnes (now represented by the Lords Say and Sele), having first mortgaged his estate to his attorney, Wm. de Ambesas. The promised co-operation of the French failed through the death of their monarch, and Edward found himself in face of the Saracen host at Nazareth, with barely a thousand men. But British valour was triumphant, and Nazareth was taken. Many of our young readers know the story of Edward's being stabbed with a poisoned dagger, and how Eleanor, his lady, sucked all the poison out of the wound without doing any harm to herself. "So sovereign a medicine," says Fuller, "is a woman's tongue, anointed with the virtue of loving affection." The valuable lives and money lavished in these enterprises is incalculable. In the year 1213, a boy in France is said to have gone about singing in his own tongue,

"Jesus, Lord, repair our loss,
Return to us Thy Holy Cross."

He was soon followed by a band of *ninety thousand children*, who never reached their destination in the Holy Land. "Their merry music soon had a sad close, all either perishing on the land, or being drowned in the sea." Thus Fuller; who, quoting from Matthew Paris, ascribes the whole movement to the devil, who, "as it were, desired a cordial of children's blood to comfort his weak stomach, long cloyed with murdering of men." Nevertheless, God's Providence brought good out of all the evil; for certainly those were days from which European civilization may date its decided progress. The general intercourse of nations emancipated men's minds from a narrow bigotry; extended

c 2

commerce; and prepared the way to receive the knowledge
of a more excellent way.

Maurice de Creon gave the Manor of Wallington, with
his daughter, to Guy le Val, who died in 1199 (1st of John),
and was succeeded by his nephew Gilbert, who was one of
the Barons that took part in securing the *Magna Charta*
for the people of England. King John's accession to the
throne of England, while Arthur, the son of his elder
brother Geoffrey, was still living, excited the amazement of
the whole nation. Thus it became necessary to secure the
popular favour by some extraordinary act; and nothing
was so likely to conciliate all parties as to promise the
restoration of those ancient liberties which had been granted
in the time. of Edward the Confessor. For, with the
Norman conquest, all had been superseded by the will of
the Sovereign. The Normans, who had at first willingly
availed themselves of the permission to seize the lands of
the Saxons, ere long became anxious lest a similar exercise
of regal power should dispossess themselves. The Forest
Laws, which denied the right of the proprietor to all game
found on his land, and which claimed "*all Beasts of Venery*"
for the King alone, were peculiarly harsh and severe.
Surrey especially seems to have suffered from those laws.
The Church, too, suffered from the withdrawal of previous
liberties. But John was not the man to yield to anything
but extreme pressure. True; John, the murderer of his
nephew Arthur, had fallen under the ban of the Pope—
Innocent III.—and on March 23rd, 1207, the whole kingdom was laid under an *Interdict*. The effect of this was;
churches were closed; the sacraments withheld, and the
dead buried, without prayers, in unconsecrated ground;

marriages were performed at the doors of the holy edifices, and prayers read in the churchyards. Misfortune had attended John in his wars in France, and of all that the English crown once possessed, Guienne only remained—so he seemed rightly named *Lackland*. Still none of these events moved him to consider his people—rather they were incitements to fresh oppressions—till in 1213 the Pope solemnly deposed John from his throne, and exhorted all Christian kings to unite against him. The French king, Philip, was rejoiced to have to put this sentence into execution, and received promises of support from some of the English Barons, whose indignation at John's conduct tempted them so far to forget themselves. Then John, finding it useless to carry on opposition, humbled himself before the Papal Legate, Pandulf, and on his knees offered him the kingdom for his lord, the Pope, with the tribute of 1,000 marks. The proud Churchman flung the money on the ground, and then stooped to pick it up—insolence and cupidity combined! All these matters aggravated the disputes between John and his Barons; till they met at Stamford at Easter, A.D. 1215, and elected *Robert Fitzwalter*, Baron of Dunmow, their leader, under the title of "Marshal of God and the Holy Church." Nor must we omit to mention the prominent part taken by *Langton*, Archbishop of Canterbury, on the side of the Barons; till at length they forced John to sign the Great Charter, at Runnemede, a meadow between Staines and Windsor, 15th of June, 1215. Twenty-five Barons were elected by the rest to enforce the observance of this instrument—the keystone of English liberty. "All that has since been obtained," says Hallam, "is little more than confirmation or commentary ; and if every subsequent law were to be swept away, there would still remain the bold features that distinguish a free from a despotic monarchy."

Since such is the fact, it is no small honor that the lord of Wallington should have joined his neighbour, William de Mowbray, of Banstead, and the other Barons, in securing this inheritance for us. But no sooner had that wretched King signed the Charter than he began to look about for objects on whom to wreak his vengeance. And so his officers seized Wallington, as forfeited by the act of its lord in opposition to the crown. John Fitz Lucy obtained a grant of it ; but he incurred a forfeiture by remaining in Normandy. The King then gave it to Eustace de Courtenay. Well might the nobles, dreading such proceedings against themselves, desire a Charter that should confirm their position. Our neighbours at Beddington were at that time no better off.

The De Watevilles had obtained full possession of the *Western* Manor in which the Church was situated. In 1159 Ingelram de Funteneys (Fontibus) and Sibyl de Wateville, sister of William de Wateville and wife of Alan Pirot, gave the advowson of the Church of Beddington to the priory of Bermondsey. In 1196 the estate had fallen into the hands of the King ; and from the Testa de Nevill, we find Richard I. gave ten shillings rent in Beddington to William de Es. His son Eustace died in 1205, and the land again reverted to the crown.

As for the other Manor in Beddington, which had come into possession of the Huscarle family, King John, in the 17th year of his reign, granted to his chaplain, Dyonisius, land which had belonged to William Huscarle. Let us pause a moment here to gather up some ideas as to those times.

Those were the days of Papal ascendancy. The Pope had blessed the banner of the Norman William when he set out to invade England. In Henry II's reign the encroachments of the Papal clergy became unbearable, assuming to themselves immunity from the laws of the realm. The Council of Clarendon (Wilts), A.D. 1164, decreed that the clergy should be tried as other men. Those were the days of Becket—educated in the monastery of our neighbouring parish, Merton. Chosen to repress the encroachments of the clergy, he became their encourager in them; till, in a hasty moment, the King exclaimed, "Will no one rid me of this proud priest?" Four gentlemen set off, and stayed not till they had taken Becket's life.

It was to Henry II. that the Pope gave Ireland; and so the green Island, the land of St. Patrick and of a true religion, became the slave of Papal superstition, and has remained in great part to the present day—"fast bound in misery and iron."

Henry, according to Papal orders, made atonement for the murder of Becket, walking barefoot and prostrating himself at the shrine, in Canterbury, of him who was now to be a SAINT Thomas. A whole day he remained fasting, and watched the relics all night; and in the morning he solemnly vowed £50 per annum for candles to illuminate the shrine. Disrobed before the monks he put a scourge in their hands ready to inflict their castigation on his bare back. Next day he received the monks' pardon, in the Pope's name.

Henry was unfortunate in his wife Eleanor, Duchess of

Aquitaine, a woman of bad character, who instigated her sons against their father; while Henry did not make matters better by his intrigue with fair Rosamond, at Woodstock. Not much wonder if John turned out so badly, trained from a child in evil ways.

But what was likely to be the character of the commonalty, if the royal palace was such? The people of Bedddington, we have seen, had been handed over to the care and teaching of the Cluniac monks of Bermondsey; Carshalton to the Austin canons of Merton, who had also a good slice of Wallington. Salmon mentions " seven parochial altars thus stripped of their dues"—all close to us. One cannot look over a few of the old monastic histories without being struck by their wealthy endowments. In the 12th century the territorial property of the Church, of which the larger part was vested in monasteries, amounted to nearly one-half of all England, and, in some countries, to a still larger proportion (Hallam.) Not that the monks had it all their own way even then, but were often lamenting the profane hand of the laity, as the hand of the wicked spoiler; just as the allocutions of Pio Nono, in our day, are full of the same distressing complaints. It is impossible to deny that, unsound in principle, the monastic system yielded, as might be expected, a harvest of mischief, not only to minds whose indolence and vice it nourished, but to pure and noble minds, whom it misled. The good it effected under an overruling Providence was, *notwithstanding* its innate corruption; and the influence it exercised on the general public was pernicious in the extreme. What could be expected from Teachers brought up in superstitious practices and immorality, such as St. Bernard, and others of themselves, describe and lament over? Truly these were the "dark ages!"—"good old times!" some would blindly affirm. But passed away now, for ever, before the light of an open gospel!

One Historical note we must not omit in reference to our Merton lords. In 1236 a Parliament, or National Council was held at Merton Abbey—whence came the Statutes of Merton. It was in this Council that the Prelacy, having introduced the Canon Law, founded on the Imperial constitutions, to supersede the common law of the realm, the Barons made the memorable declaration: "Nolumus leges Angliæ mutare"—"We will not alter the laws of England." The Inquisition was established at the beginning of the 13th century. One of the Albigenses, first opponents of Rome, was burnt in London A.D. 1210. Thirty Germans had suffered at Oxford in 1168

But a greater power than Pope or Prelate, Barons, or any National Councils, was about to make itself felt in England. The morning star of the Reformation at length arose to shine on our land; and Wicliff stood forth to proclaim "the naughty deeds of the Friars," and the mysterious "Beast." Yet we must pass the stirring and not inglorious times of Edward I. and III., as affording no "Historical Notes" for *Wallington*. From the days of King John, the Manor had passed through the families of Salinis and de la Lynde, till we find Katharine, widow of Thomas Lodelawe, died siesed of this Manor in 1394, 17th of Richard the Second. This was just eleven years after Wicliff had completed his trans-lation—the first—of the whole Bible into English, and his followers had become known as "Lollards," "the singers" of Psalms and Hymns, such as St. Paul encouraged

(Col. iii. 16). Bible Printing had not then come in. But a hundred years after, Dr. Roland Phillips, Vicar of Croydon, preaching at St. Paul's, London, exclaimed, " We (meaning the Romanists) must root out printing, or printing will root out us."

But as we have some notes of transactions in Beddington, we will give them, ere we close the 14th century. After the days of King John, the Manor of Home-Beddington, or Westcourt, was granted to Raymund de Laik, or Lucas, in 1238. A Lucas was Archdeacon of Surrey, and Sub-deacon of the Pope. In the reign of Edward I., the Manor fell to the King, who granted it to Thomas Corbet, his valet ! It afterwards passed to Thomas De Merle ; then to Thomas de Brayton, clerk ; and finally to Richard de Wyloghby, or Willoughby. Sir Rd. de Wyloghby had an only daughter, Lucy, who married first Sir Thomas Huscarle, who held then the other Manor of Beddington, which he had held in King John's time. [The Huscarle seems (as the name denotes, *House Steward*), to have been an old Saxon family. In "Domesday" such a name occurs at Abinger, Surrey]. Sir Thos. Huscarle died, and his widow married Nicolas de Carreu, who thus became possessed of the two manors.

There was apparently, for a time, another Manor of " Bandon," over which Edmund, Earl of Cornwall, claimed seignorial jurisdiction in 1279 ; and early in the reign of Edward III. Reginald le Forester held a messuage and 30 acres of land in Bandon and Beddington of Thomas Corbet. This le Forester was Sheriff in 1344 ; M.P. for Surrey in 1348. There was an estate here belonging to the Hospital of St. Thomas, Southwark, called the Manor of Freres, Friars, or Brethren ; and, in 1353, the Archbishop of

Nazareth had a bit of Beddington. Did he come over to this country with Edward I. on his return from Palestine, as the friend of Edward's valet? In those days there was also one Simon Roke, citizen skinner of London, who held land in Bedyngton, Bandon, Wodecote and Waletone. Woodcote appears generally apart from the rest. Is it identical with Rd. de Tonbridge's holding in "Domesday?"

Having mentioned St. Thomas' Hospital, it may be interesting to trace its history, as in connection with our neighbourhood. It was in 1213 that Richard, the then Prior of Bermondsey—in whom the advowson of Beddington was invested since A.D. 1159—" an old hospital for the maintenance of the poor, long since built, having been destroyed by fire and utterly reduced to ashes"—proposed to build a new one adjoining the Priory, and dedicate it to St. Thomas (à Becket). The then Bishop of Winchester supported the plan, granting an indulgence for thirty days to all persons who should contribute. On the suppression of monasteries, a well-timed sermon by Ridley, Bishop of London, awakened the benevolence of the young king, Edward VI; and after consultation with the Lord Mayor and Corporation, three great charitable institutions were decided on—*Christ's Hospital*, for the education of youth; *Bridewell*, for the poor, and correcting the profligate; and *St. Thomas'*, for the relief of the lame and sick. What an amount of good has been effected by means of these and similar institutions throughout our land, founded by the saintly youth, Edward VI—turning possessions which had mainly nourished superstition, into sources of healing of the mind and body! In July, 1552, the city began to repair and enlarge the Hospital, and in the November

following, 260 poor and infirm people were received into it.
The Hospital has suffered greatly in its possessions, though
not in its buildings, by the fires of 1676, 1681, and 1689.
A new building was commenced in 1692; and now on a
different site, opposite Westminster, on the Thames S.
Embankment, there has been erected another building, or
seven separate ones, supplying 600 beds for patients—an
Institution whose benefits the people of Wallington, in our
day, often experience.

The Nicholas de Carew who first came to our neighbourhood was of an ancient family.* In 1362 he was one of
the Knights of the Shire for Surrey. In 1372 he was
made Keeper of the Privy-Seal by Edward III., who likewise appointed him one of his executors. He died in 1391,
about which time the greater part of the present Beddington
Church was built; towards which he left £20.

There is a silver penny "such as is usually ascribed to
Edward II." (as Mr. Poole, of the British Museum, has
kindly given his opinion)—not Edward I—in the Museum
at Beddington School, which was "found under the foun-
dation of the N.W. pillar of the nave of Beddington Church,

---

* Manning (vol. ii) traces the pedigree of the Carew family from Otho
who came originally from Florence, and then with Wm. I., to England.
His residence was at Stanwell, Middlesex. His son Walter married a
North Wales Princess, and was made Governor of Windsor Castle; whence
his family were called "de Windsor," "Lords Windsor"—now in the
Clive family. A grandson married a South Wales Princess, and, through
her, the family had Carrio Castle, properly Caerew—the "fortress"
(Collins), Pembrokeshire. The same grandson had a grant of Moulsford,
Berks., from Henry I. Sir William, in time of John, was the first that
appears with the name of Carru (A.D. 1213). From Sir Nicholas, of
Moulsford (who died in 1308), descended four sons: (1st) Sir John,
ancestor of the Carews, of Cornwall; (3rd) Nicholas, who came to
Beddington.

July, 1850;" so Rev. Jas. Hamilton testifies. Curious are those silver pennies of the time of the Edwards—difficult to distinguish from one another, but easily recognized in themselves; as an old versifier—

> "Edward did smite round penny, halfpenny, farthing;
> The cross passeth the bond of all, throughout the ring:
> The king's side, whereon his name written.
> The cross side, what city it was in coined and smitten.
> To poor man ne to priest, the penny frays nothing;
> Men give God aye the least—they feof (endow) him with a farthing.
> A thousand, two hundred, fourscore years and mo,
> On this money men wondered, when it first began to go."

There are four such pennies in the Museum of Bedding-ton School, besides coins of later date.

Before the Church was arranged in the present manner—of which hereafter—the organ was in the Tower; and "in the singer's gallery, which partly occupies the space behind the organ, were four old wooden stalls, having turn-up seats, or 'miseries,' ornamented with foliage, shields, a female head in a reticulated head-dress, and other carvings." It seems probable that the above stalls were originally provided for the "four fit Chaplains," which Nicholas de Carreu in his will, dated in 1387, directs "should be found, one of them for ever, and the others for five years; to pray for his soul, and all Christian souls, in the Church at Beddington." (Brayley, 1844.) But he knew not the days of such mass-priests were even then numbered. The "will" also contained provision for "12 torches, and 5 wax tapers, each weighing at most 6 lbs.," for the funeral. But he could not have passed from Wales to Ireland, as some of his family did, or he would have known the Irish blessing: "May every hair in your head be a candle to light you to

glory !" and then this part of the will of that rich and
" accomplished man" would have been different? However,
his better sense appears in making provision for the clothing of 13 poor men to carry the torches.

Thus having placed Beddington under the Carews, in
whose family the greater part of the Parish continued till
1856, we will return home to Wallington. In 1314, one
Thomas de Lodelowe died siesed of the manor of Tooting ;
and his son's widow dying in 1394, the inheritance, *with
the manor of Wallington*, devolved on his daughter Margaret,
the wife of Sir John Dymock, whose family held Tooting
and Wallington for nearly two centuries—till the time of
Elizabeth (Brayley). It seems from the records of Merton
Priory, they held their principal Manor Court at *Micham;*
and Sir John Dymock received at his Court, at *Waleton*, suit
and fealty for lands held of him in the Parish of Kingston.
We may suppose that the principal residence of the Dymock
family was at Wallington. Manning gives an extract from
the "Close Rolls," stating that in 1454, the family of Sir
Thos. Greene held lands in *Waylyngton* and Woodmarston.
Does this mean *Woodcote?*

In Burke's "Landed Gentry," we are told that the family
Dymock derived its name from Dymock, in Gloucestershire ;
and they have inherited Scrivelsby, county Lincoln, from
the Baronial House of Marmion.

> "They hailed him lord of Fontenaye,
>   Of Luterwarde and Scrivelbaye,
>   Of Tamworth tower and town."—
>   SCOTT'S MARMION—Canto I.

The lords Marmion claimed to be hereditary Champions
to the Dukes of Normandy, and so of the English sover-

cigns. Philip de Marmion, in Henry III. had four daughters. Joan, who had for her portion the manor of Scrivelsby, married Sir Thos. de Lodelowe, Knt. Their daughter and sole heiress, Margaret, married Sir John Dymock; thence of Wallington.

The first of the Dymock family who was officially employed as Champion, was this Sir John, at the coronation of Richard II. Sir Baldwin Freville claimed the office of Champion, but it was adjudged to the Dymock family, in whose family it is now hereditary. The office of Champion is "to ride completely armed upon a barbed horse into Westminster Hall, and then to challenge combat with whomsoever there should be, who should dare to oppose the Sovereign's title to the crown."

Sir Thos. Dymock, in reign of Edward IV., gave way to the temptation of joining Lord Welles—a family connection —and the Lancastrian party, and suffered a premature death on the scaffold. Perhaps this accounts for a note in Manning, that Sir Nicholas Carew had the "forfeited" (?) Manor of Wallington from Henry VIII? and on the attainder of this Carew, the Manor was recovered by the Dymocks.

Sir Edward Dymock was Champion at the coronation of Edward VI. and Mary, and also of Queen Elizabeth. He died in 1566, and was succeeded by his son Robert; whose son, Sir Edward Dymock, married Catharine, daughter of Sir James Harington; and so was purchased, from the Dymock family, this Manor of Wallington in 1592, which was again transferred in 1596 to Sir Francis Carew.

The Haringtons, though not long connected with Wallington, are a remarkable family in this period of English history; so we will refer to some "Notes" in reference to them, There were two families of Haringtons in Queen Elizabeth's time—one, Sir John Harington's, who was godson of the Queen, whose place was at Kelston (Somerset), now of Wendon, Devonshire. He was distinguished for his wit and gallantry, and was accounted the Martial of his day. The other family, which was connected with Wallington, trace their origin and name to Haverington, in the county of Cumberland, and eventually they settled at Exton, in Rutlandshire. The then Sir James Harington, of Exton, Knt., dying in 1592, left three sons—John, Henry, and James.

1. JOHN, created in 1603 Baron Harington, of Exton, was tutor to the Princess Elizabeth, daughter of James I., and went with her, as her guardian, on her marriage to the Count Palatine—Fred. V.—and died at Worms in 1613. The daughter of this Princess was Sophia, from whom our present royal dynasty of Hanover.

3. JAMES, whose grandson, Sir James Harington, was M.P. for the county of Middlesex in 1654, and one of the Commissioners for trying King Charles I; and after the Restoration was, with Lord Castlemaine, Sir Henry Mildmay and others, excepted out of the general pardon. The first cousin, of this last, was James Harington, groom of the bed-chamber to Charles I., and who attended his Sovereign to the scaffold. He was educated at Trinity College, Oxford, by Chillingworth, the gifted author of "The Religion of Protestants;" and was himself the author of *The Commonwealth of Oceana*—"a political allegory, which exhibited, in a fictitious land, the form of government most conducive to public liberty." It was a book which created

much excitement by its publication in those days. Cromwell said, in reference to it, that he " would not suffer himself to be scribbled out of what he had won with his sword;" and even now, the great Journal of our *Times*—in the day of grace, 1872—quotes "Oceana" in its arguments. However, the Harington family have left sundry small legacies behind them, for the benefit of Wallington, in the shape of some *farthing-tokens of copper*, picked up in the fields at various times—a coinage then, for the first time since the days of the Heptarchy, introduced into England. The farthings we read of previously were one of the pieces of a silver penny cut into four. Proposals for such pieces had been made to Elizabeth, who resolutely refused to listen to any scheme for a copper currency. But in James I., John Harington—Baron Exton—was empowered to make them : hence they were called, in the slang of the day, "Haringtons." There are some fifteen of them in the School Museum. "Their type is two sceptres crossed in saltier—one surmounted by a cross, the other by a *fleur-de-lis;* above, a crown; legend, JACO. D. G. MAG. BRIT. Reverse : an Irish harp crowned, FRA. ET. HIB. REX."

Having arrived at a period of our History when Wallington no longer had an independent existence as a separate Manor, we turn to the common fount of honour to Beddington and Wallington—the Carew family. From the time of their entry into our neighbourhood, they exercised a considerable influence, and, ere long, became possessors of the greater portion of the landed property in 18 parishes of the county.

We take up our "Historical Notes" again with the commencement of the 15th century ; and we find successive

D

Carews *representing* the county in several Parliaments, or
as *Sheriffs* of the county. In the *Carew Chapel,* in Beddington Church, are several interesting monuments—the
oldest being that of the founder, Sir Richard Carew, made
a Knight Banneret at the battle of Blackheath, in 1497,
when the people of Cornwall rose against the increased
taxation, and, headed by Lord Audley, marched towards
London, and, on Blackheath, suffered a signal defeat. Sir
Nicholas, son and heir of Sir Richard, was a great favorite
with Henry VIII., and was, for several years, the almost
constant companion of the king, " and a partaker with him
in all the jousts, tournaments, masques, and other diversions
with which that reign abounded." Yet, notwithstanding
these and many other honours received from his Sovereign,
he appears to have engaged in a conspiracy with the
Marquis of Exeter; Henry Pole, Lord Montacute; Sir Edwd.
Neville; the then Rector of Beddington, his relative; and
others (all zealous Roman Catholics), to overthrow the
Government, and set Cardinal Pole upon the throne. The plot
was discovered by the agency of a brother of one of the con-
spirators, and all were executed. Sir Nicholas was beheaded
on Tower Hill, A.D. 1539, when he made "a godly confession
of his fault and his superstitious faith," (Holinshed). His
estates were forfeited; but his only son, Sir Francis, being
in the service of Queen Mary, obtained the restitution of
his ancestral inheritance in 1554. This gentleman erected
a magnificent mansion at Beddington, in which he had the
honour of being twice visited by Queen Elizabeth. [There
was a Manor House before, for Henry VIII. held a council
there in 1541.]

Doubtless the son had fully realized the folly of his

father, and could clearly see what his father could not, "that no foreign prince, prelate, or potentate hath, or ought to have, pre-eminence or authority in this realm of England." One wonders what were his feelings when, on the 27th of November, 1554, at a special sitting of Parliament, Pole sat on the right of the Queen, wearing his Cardinal's hat, promising the Pope's blessing, if the nation would again submit to him; and only one member, Sir Ralph Bagnall, stood firm to his principles, and refused to kneel before the Pope's representative. Sir Francis died unmarried in 1611. There is a costly monument to this Carew—a fine example of the sepulchral style of James I. It is a long altar-tomb, upon which, between two Corinthian columns of black marble, supporting an enriched entablature, lies a full-length statue of the deceased, sculptured in alabaster, upon a mat. He is represented in complete armour with a skull-cap, instead of a helmet: his hands are as in prayer. In front of the tomb, on a low plinth, and kneeling upon cushions, are small figures of a Knight in armour, and his lady in a ruff and long cloak, together with five sons and two daughters—the latter wearing ruffs and farthingales. These, as we learn from an affixed tablet, represent Sir Nicholas Throckmorton (his nephew, who succeeded to his estates, and who erected this monument "to the memorie of his deare and well deserving unckle"); Mary, his wife, eldest daughter of Sir Geo. More, of Losely, Knt., and their seven children. Sir Nicholas Throckmorton, like his father, was a zealous Protestant and earnest Christian. The inscription, therefore, becomes such a man; and though somewhat laudatory of his "unckle," tells us that "Christ alone was his hope in his last hours"—a great

D 2

contrast to the first of the Beddington Carews, as previously
noted. His father was celebrated both as a soldier and a
statesman; and acquired so much of the royal favour of
Queen Elizabeth, that the Earl of Leicester is suspected to
have hastened his death by poison, "as he died suddenly
at the Earl's house, near Temple Bar, after eating a hearty
supper, 1570." He had a residence in Carshalton; and
one would be curious to know what father and son would
have thought of that Vicar of Carshalton, *W. Quelche, B.D.*,
who would have himself commemorated as one whose " lott
was, through God's mercy, to burne incense here about
30 yr., and ended his covrse April 10, Ano. Dni. 1654,
being aged 64 years." Sir Nicholas (the son) must have
felt sorely grieved during the last twenty years of his life
with this curiosity in his native Parish, if he was really
one of the Laudian revivalists, and attempting to use incense
as part of the ceremonial of the Church of England, which
it is not, nor of the true Catholic Church. If the wise men
brought among their gifts, frankincense, they did not burn
it. Indeed, as Dr. Hook says, " The use of incense, in
connection with the Eucharist, was unknown in the Church
until the time of Gregory the Great, in the latter part of
the sixth century." But we will hope the Vicar Quelch
was only giving a figurative expression to his sentimentality
on behalf of the *ashes!* (save the Christian *body!*) of a
certayne fryer, his predecessor in the Vicarage, and was
neither Pope nor Pagan. Yet in 1624, there was placed on
the floor of the S. aisle in Carshalton Church, on a brass
plate, the figure of a woman praying; and out of her mouth
comes this inscription :—

"O blessed Lady of pittie, p'y for me, y^t my soule savy'd may be."

And underneath again : "Pray for the soule of Johan Burton, on whose soule Jhu have mercy. Amen."

In Beddington Church we have other fashions. Margaret Huntley, wife of John Huntley, who lived at *Wallington Place* (according to Sir Francis Carew's will, 1611), was buried 1638, "in certain hope of a joyful resurrection :" "virtus post funera vivit." Over this is a death's head ; below is winged hour-glass ; and on each side is a skeleton —singular ideas as to emblems of joy, one would say. But in the same Church, Mr. Greenhill (see epitaph), a Master of Arts, in 1633, exhibited a tablet with similar ornaments. So Beddington led Wallington then; for "examples are catching."

All this puts one very much in mind of the little excrescenses to the Churches one sees on the Continent, in the shape of little chapels filled with human bones; sometimes with figures of men and women rising up out of what appears to be the flames of hell, and evil spirits keeping them in fire. Doubtless, useful incitements to the faithful that they should pay the mass-priest to pray them out.

But we are getting on over fast, some may say, if we leave out all notice of "good Queen Bess," who so favoured our liege lord of that day with her visits. Is it possible that some of that Queen's loyal subjects were not always so pleased with those Progresses, as were the proprietors of the mansions she honoured by her presence ? For whenever the Court moved, in the neighbourhood, a grand embargo was laid on horses and conveyances for the use of Her Majesty ; and this happening frequently, was no light burden. As many as 24,000 horses are said to have been required on some occasions to move Elizabeth's household from the county in which she had been residing.

The vicinity of Nonsuch Palace, in the Parish of Cheam
—or rather Cuddington—made these visits easy. The
Manor of Cuddington came into possession of the crown in
1539. The old Mansion and Parish Church were pulled
down, and two parks inclosed; and shortly afterwards the
King commenced the erection of the Palace of " *Nonesuch*."
The works were not completed on the death of the King,
in 1547. In 1557 Queen Mary granted it for a sum of
money, and in exchange for Manors in Norfolk, to the Earl
of Arundel; from whom it passed to Lord Lumley, from
whom Queen Elizabeth purchased it, and passed much of
her time there during the summer season. It was at
Nonsuch that the Earl of Essex had a remarkable interview
with Her Majesty on his return from Ireland in Sept.
1599. James I. settled Nonsuch on his Queen, Anne of
Denmark. During the Commonwealth the property passed
through various hands, till the Queen Dowager, Henrietta
Maria, recovered possession, about 1660. In July, 1665,
when the plague raged in London, sweeping off about
100,000 people, the Exchequer Court was removed for a
time to the " Queene's House," at Nonsuch. It seems as if,
that year, the plague did not reach this neighbourhood, as
there are no deaths from it recorded at' Carshalton or
Beddington; although, in 1625, there were 11 deaths at
Beddington. The royal profligate, Charles II., granted
Nonsuch to the notorious Barbara, created Baroness Nonsuch, Countess of Southampton, Duchess of Cleveland.
Having obtained possession, she pulled down the Palace of
Nonsuch, sold the materials, and divided the Parks into
farms.

Till the reign of Queen Elizabeth, there were few "*country houses*" with any comforts. There were grand, gloomy castles, with narrow windows; but large windows were the cheerful characteristics that the Elizabethan style introduced. Rushes for covering the floors began then to be discontinued; the lower classes used sand; the middle and upper ranks had their floors polished, and sometimes inlaid with different coloured woods; and carpets, or pieces of tapestry, were laid down in different parts of the room. The orders of John Haryngton's household in 1566 direct, that "the hall be made clean every day, by eight in winter, and seven in summer." (The hall was the principal apartment, where the family dependents all took their meals together, sitting at different tables according to their rank.) "All stairs in the house, and rooms that need shall require, were to be made clean on Fridays, after dinner. When any stranger departed, his chamber was to be drest up again within four hours after." "The meat for dinner was to be ready by eleven, and for supper at six or seven in the evening."

One little note we must give. During the reign of Elizabeth, fair hair became fashionable; and the ladies, therefore, used various compositions for dyeing their locks this attractive colour; and even fair-haired children were enticed into corners and feloniously polled, that court head-dresses might be made from the spoil. The statute of 23rd of Henry VIII. seems to have had little effect: "Every temporal person, whose *wife* shall wear any gown or petti-coat of silk, or any French hood, or bonnet of velvet, or any chain of gold about the neck, should keep one trotting horse for saddle, able for warres, of 3 yrs. or more, and 14

hands high." Who would submit to be taxed according to
his wife's dress, in our day?

The *progresses* of Queen Elizabeth have been fully noted
by Nicholls, to whom we must refer the curious for full
particulars in these matters. When the Queen visited
Kenilworth, there were consumed, of beer alone, three
hundred and twenty hogsheads. In her progress to Lord
Montacute's, three oxen and a hundred and forty geese were
eaten at a single breakfast. Twelve times she visited her
favourite statesman at Theobald's, and each visit cost Cecil
between two and three thousand pounds.

However, those were grand days for England. Elizabeth
may have had her weaknesses, but she had, withal, the sense
to choose excellent Ministers of State; and the advance of
England, during her reign, was great indeed in intellectual
and material subjects; while the consolidating influence of
true religion was a guarantee for real progress afterward.

During Mary's reign of five years, nearly 300 persons
were burnt for adherence to the Reformed faith; twenty-six
in Surrey and Sussex (of whom Brayley gives the names).
All the Romeward feelings and acts of Elizabeth's predecessor, failed to change the heart of English nation. Of
some 10,000 parish ministers, scarcely 200 refused to
accept the principles of the Reformation under Elizabeth.
Hallam endorses the words, in which Carte sums up the
character of Elizabeth's unlamented predecessor, as perfectly
just: "Having reduced the nation to the brink of ruin,
she left it, by her seasonable decease, to be restored by her
successor to its ancient prosperity and glory." The
thunders of the Papal Court against the Protestant Queen,
and the attempts of foreign powers, only served to exhibit

the loyalty of Queen and People to each other; and the medal struck in commemoration of the defeat of the "Invincible Armada," with its inscription, "Deus afflavit et dissipantur," was a suitable acknowledgment of Divine Providence. And now began to stand forth a galaxy of imperishable names, which made this century remarkable.

But while under James I. the nation made rapid advances in wealth and intelligence; and trade and maritime enterprise flourished—witness Sir Walter Raleigh, married to a Carew—causes were at work, which led to a great national convulsion in the next reign. Laud and Strafford are made to bear the blame in their respective departments of Church and State; but the untruthfulness of Charles, together with his arrogant assumptions of the Divine right of kings, contributed mainly to his own downfall. The struggle for popular rights resulted in much suffering to landowners and clergy, of which last class, thousands were deprived of their means of living, and prohibited from exercising their sacred functions. Eventually a military despotism prepared the people to welcome the Restoration of royalty, on almost any terms. Nevertheless, Cromwell ruled the kingdom with vigour and distinguished ability; English influence was felt far and wide, on the side of truth and justice. Thus, always, unselfish English sympathy loves to show itself. We might instance his interference on behalf of the Valdese inhabitants of the Italian Alps, under their persecuting Sovereign. Milton's immortal lines recur :—

ON THE LATE MASSACRE IN PIEMONT.

Avenge, O Lord, thy slaughtered saints, whose bones
      Lie scatter'd on the Alpine mountains cold;
      Even them who kept thy truth so pure of old,
      When all our fathers worshipped stocks and stones,
Forget not; in thy book record their groans
      Who were thy sheep, and in their ancient fold
      Slain by the bloody Piemontese, that roll'd
      Mother with infant down the rocks. The moans
The vales redoubled to the hills, and they
      To heaven. Their martyred blood and ashes sow
      O'er all the Italian fields, where still doth sway
The triple tyrant; that from these may grow
      A hundredfold, who, having learnt thy way,
      Early may fly the Babylonian woe.

Prophetic words! which are receiving fulfilment in the evangelizing efforts of the Valdese throughout Italy, still supported for their *Home-Parishes* among the Alps, by a fund arising out of a national contribution made in England, with Cromwell's authority, over £32,000. The Protector himself gave £,2000. The cities of London and Westminster, £9,384 6s. 11d.

Our neighbourhood was not destitute of such feelings; as we read in the Beddington " Church Book," that not only were there collections on a brief for St. Paul's Cathedral, 6th October, 1678, to be re-built by Sir C. Wren; when the Carew of that day promised £5 for three years; the Rector £1 for two years; but in 1681 and 1682, collections made towards the relief of the French Protestants, £2 3s. 9½d., and £10 9s. 0d.

The Massacre of St. Bartholomew, in 1572, stamped as it was with the approval of the Pope, Gregory XIII, "drunk with the blood of the saints," (Rev. xvii. 6), by his medal, "*Ugonottorum*, 1572," had only whetted the depraved appetite of "the most Christian King" and nation of France. The very exodus of the best of the land, to more hospitable shores, carrying with them so much of the nation's commercial industry, only roused the more bitter feelings against the Huguenots. "Honest as a Huguenot" had passed into a proverb. But it was in France, as of old: "I hate him," said the Athenian, "for all men speak well of Aristides." In 1681 the Protestant University of *Sedan* was arbitrarily closed by Louis XVIII. Elizabeth had given a free asylum in England to the persecuted French Huguenots. In 1625, Charles I., with the aid of his minister, Buckingham, equipped an English fleet to take part against the Huguenots, then besieged by the French King in La Rochelle—falsely pretending another object. But as soon as the true destination was learnt, captains and men refused to be tricked into such a shameful scheme; and repeated attempts of Charles and his minister were in vain to make English sailors take the side of falsehood against God's truth. Be it ever so! And though Charles II. was a Romanist at heart, he was constrained by public opinion, in 1681, to sanction legal enactments in favour of such refugees as should reach our shores. A newspaper of the day announces: Plymouth, 6th Sept., 1681, "an open boat arrived here yesterday, in which were 40 or 50 Protestants who resided outside La Rochelle." Large numbers also arrived at Dover, Rye, etc.—many Pastors, hungering and in rags. At Rye, 18th April, 1682, Wm. Williams, the Vicar, and others, drew up a testimonial in favour of the refugees, and allowed the use of the Parish Church for their services. About that time many French Protestants settled at Wandsworth, and engaged in trade there, and had a Chapel of their own. How like they to Abram in his pilgrimage, building an altar wherever he stayed (Gen. xii). · Why should not English people do likewise in foreign lands?

It was Michaelmas, 1683, when the troublous times of the Commonwealth were well nigh forgotten, and the wasted years of Charles II. were closing in darkness, amid wars abroad and plots at home, that Sir Nicholas Carew found it necessary to make over Wallington, and several estates in adjoining parishes, to Robert Spencer, Anthony Bowyer, and John Spencer, for a term of 500 years; in trust that they should dispose of the property for the benefit of the younger portion of his family—six children. The era of the Revolution succeeded, and so the business was delayed; till, ultimately, an agreement was made for the sale of "Wallington Place," for the above-named term, to William Bridges, of the Tower of London, Surveyor-General of the Ordnance, and M.P. for Liskeard. (His portrait at the Manor House, with a roll in hand.) His great-grandfather was a gentleman of an old family in Ireland, who in A.D. 1578, settled at Alcester, in Warwickshire. An uncle lived at Harcourt Hall, in Worcestershire, and distinguished himself as Col. John Bridges, during the Civil Wars. He was a firm friend of Richard Baxter, of the same county, in whose life he is mentioned with honour. He used all his influence in favour of faithful ministers of the gospel; and several works of the Puritans are dedicated to him—as "Trapp on the Gospels," and "Baxter's Peace of Conscience."

Col. Bridges at first sided with Lord Brook, Hampden, and Cromwell against the encroachments of the Crown.

He lived at Edsom Hall, near Alcester. But we have no record where he was on that Sunday, 23rd October, 1642, when Baxter was preaching in the village of Alcester, and the roaring of cannon was announcing the battle of Edgehill. We are told the thunder of the battle disturbed neither the preacher nor the congregation. Was it the eloquence of the great Puritan preacher that entranced his hearers, and suspended their alarm? It was the first battle fought on English soil for centuries. The parishioners of Alcester then were not trained for war; but they had learnt the noble lesson of peace, in the midst of danger—in a word, to put their trust in God. In the following year, 1643, Col. Bridges was Governor of Warwick Castle, and continued Governor almost all the time of the war. Afterwards he lived near Kidderminster, being Patron of the Church, a Justice of Peace, and a Parliament man. But, seeing the danger of Republicanism, gradually he changed his opinions, and ultimately sided with the party who restored the exiled Royal family. Then he lived in Ireland, where his family had property; and, with others, surprised Dublin Castle and Sir Hardress Waller, for the King, effecting his object skilfully, without bloodshed.

The present Lord of the Manor of Wallington is descended from his eldest son John, who married Elizabeth, sister of Sir Wm. Trumbull, one of the Secretaries of State to King William III., whose epitaph Pope wrote, and some of whose correspondence with Pope has been preserved in the family, and appears in a late edition of that Poet's works. Then, doubtless, Pope could describe, from personal observation, "the blue transparent Vandalis," and had tasted the "mutton from Banstead Down," while "Dame Bridges" was resident at the Manor House. Though we should observe that the proverb does not allow all the honours to Banstead. It ran :

Sutton for mutton; Carshalton for beves;
Epsom for salts (?); Ewell for thieves.—GROSE, 1811.

Lodgings at Epsom Spa were fashionable and dear. So the light-fingered gentry sought cheaper accommodation in Ewell, whence to sally forth to the prey in Epsom.

Brooke, the second son of Col. Bridges—godson of Lord Brook, that staunchest of Patriots and Puritan of Puritans —was the father of Sir Brook Bridges, of Goodnestone, the first Baronet, one of the Auditors of the Treasury (A.D. 1718). From him is descended the present Lord Fitzwalter, better known, hitherto, as Sir Brook Wm. Bridges, as staunch in the cause of Evangelical and Protestant truth, as ever was his illustrious "name-father," only, as a truer patriot, loyal to his Sovereign. He has claimed also, and been allowed by the House of Peers, to be Senior co-heir, through the female line, of the Baron Fitzwalter, of King John's time. We have little to note of the times of the "Glorious Revolution," except to add the name of another soldier in this family—Sir Matthew Bridges—who distinguished himself under William III., and also under Marlborough, but was killed before Maestricht in 1703. There is a fine portrait of him in his uniform of that period; as there is of Col. Bridges, Sir Wm. Trumbull and his lady, and of Sir Brook Bridges, the Auditor (painted by *Lely*).

The first of the Bridges family who resided at Wallington was Elizabeth, the sister and sole heiress of Wm. Bridges, above, who died in 1714. She had also her town house in

Soho Square. **Madam Bridges** seems to have been a singular old lady, of the strong-minded order. Among many other tales, an old man, in 1804, related that she had a habit of perambulating the boundaries of Wallington in a coach and four, which he remembered being driven through a stream, forming one boundary of the Manor; and across the stream she used to throw, out of her coach, buns to the children who stood on her side of the stream. Pleasanter treatment than being bumped against the walls of our School-room, to make one remember which were the proper Parish limits, on occasion of the annual Perambulation of the Boundaries of Wallington and Carshalton! There is a portrait of this lady in the old Manor House. She, dying in 1745, left her property in strict entail. One of her successors, a nephew, became Sir Bridges Baldwin, High Sheriff of Surrey in 1760. Afterwards, **Mr. William Bridges** inherited. His portrait represents him with a flute. He, too, was a great curiosity. He is described by our oldest inhabitant as "a little old gentleman, who liked great things." His early life had been spent in Italy; and so when he came into possession (which he retained for thirty years), he put an Italian front to the old structure. He had a great housekeeper, and he drove about in a great coach (he never mounted a horse), wore a cocked hat, bagwig, and great buckles in his shoes. He had a large fur tippet over his shoulder; a muff for his hands, when it was cold, and a sunshade for his complexion, when it was hot. When he walked abroad in this dress, with a velvet cap on his head, he seemed to be the terror of all the little boys and girls of the Parish. This is that Mr. Wm. Bridges who left £200 in the 3 per cent. Consols—the interest to

be for the benefit of the poor of Wallington. He died
unmarried in 1805, and was buried at Beddington. He
divided his property between the descendants of the Col.
John Bridges, above—now represented by Mr. N. Bridges
—and a branch of the family of Lord Fitzwalter; now
represented by the Rev. Thos. Pym Bridges, of Danbury,
Essex. The first in the succession to Wallington should
have been Nathaniel Bridges, D.D., some time Lecturer of
St. Mary, Redcliff, Bristol, where he lies buried—not
forgotten. But the little old gentleman, expressing in a
codicil, doubts of his relative's fitness to occupy the place of
the Lord of the Manor of Wallington, passed him over in
favour of his younger brother; and left him to carry on a
higher work, which his sorrowing people have recorded in
an epitaph to his memory :—

> " Marbles shall moulder, monuments decay,
>   Time sweep memorials from the earth away ;
>   But lasting records are to Bridges given,
>   The letters adamant, the archives heaven.
>   There living records of his worth engraved
>   Stand fast for ever—in the souls he saved."

We will now endeavour to recall the state of Wallington
and the neighbourhood in that day, with the aid vouchsafed
to us, out of special favour, by the oldest inhabitants; and
so bring it down to our own day. We shall, of course, first
have something to say about the Church. For there was
then a building answering to this description. Manning,
taking from Lysons, describes it : " In a field, near the
" road, are the remains of a small Church or Chapel, built
" of flints and stone, the walls of which are for the most
" part entire, but it is now made use of as an Outhouse to

" the adjoining Farm. This was probably no other than a
" Chapel of Ease to the Church of Beddington, there being
" no Church at Wallington in the time of the *General*
" *Survey* (Domesday). It was new roofed a few years ago.
" The stone work of the windows is entire. The East win-
" dow has been stopped up; on each side of it is a niche of
" rich Gothic architecture; and in the South-east corner is
" a third for the holy water." Mr. Lysons could find no
record in the Registry of Winchester concerning this
structure. It stood on the rising ground, above Mr. Boorne's
Brewery; on land which formed part of the Manor House
property, but is now with the Elm Grove Estate. It was
pulled down in 1791. Mr. Smee, in " My Garden," states,
in reference to the site, he had seen " tons of stones there
piled together; and one piece, evidently a stone of a window
or door of a first-class Gothic edifice. There were numerous
other fragments of tooled stones."

That Wallington had some ecclesiastical standing, seems
borne out by the fact that at the Visitation of the Clergy,
the Benefice is entitled "Beddington-cum-Wallington,"
which is not consistent with the idea that the Hamlet of
Wallington, supporting its own poor, levying its own
rates, etc., independently; is only a *civil* distinction, and not
ecclesiastical. Other Parishes composed of more than one
district, similarly independent of each other in civil matters,
have no similar record of their distinct existence noted in
ecclesiastical matters; and people did sometimes pull down
Churches, without re-building them—as Cuddington Church
was pulled down to make way for Nonesuch Palace; and so
it is Cheam-cum-Cuddington.

It has been argued by those who should know something

E

of these matters, that there was a part of the Tithes of Beddington, set apart for the parson of Wallington. Is this likely in the nature of things? The origin of Parishes and Tithes is opposed to this, unless as an exceptional case.

If we go back to "hoar antiquity," the tithes of Wallington, not of Beddington, should support the parson of Wallington. Let us recall a few facts connected with the History of our English Parishes. How the Gospel came to our shores, it is needless to enquire. Whether the *Claudia* and *Pudens*, of 2 Tim. iv. 21, were ever numbered among the British Christians, we will not argue. (See Conybeare and Howson in "Life of St. Paul.") But *Linus*, of the same Epistle, was a Briton, afterwards a Bishop of Rome. Caractacus was a fellow-prisoner at Rome, with Paul, A.D. 50. We have the memory of one British martyr in the faith of Christ, preserved in the name of St. Alban's, Hertfordshire. The mild sway of Constantius Chlorus would temper the Diocletian edicts of persecution; and the Gospel advanced again. So that when the Emperor Constantine summoned an Ecclesiastical Council at Arles, A.D. 314, three British Bishops attended—from York, London, and Caerleon. We have also good reason to believe there were also British Bishops at Nice (A.D. 325), when Constantine called together that Council, as there were at Sardica, in 347, and Ariminum, in 349. The invasion of the Saxons created sad havoc in the Church of Britain; and ere long it was restricted to the remote parts of the Island; to Cornwall, Wales, Cumberland, and Scotland. But when the monk, Augustine, came, there were traces everywhere of what had been. The Church he is described as building at Canterbury, was on the ruins of an old British Church.

History tells us of conferences he held, with British Bishops, and his controversies with them as to their mode of keeping Easter, and celebrating Baptism which was according to *Eastern* mode—not the Roman. It were too long a tale to tell; but it is clearly proved that the recovery of the Island to Christianity, was mainly due to the efforts of the Ancient British Church; aroused, indeed, to duty by Augustine and his Roman friends. Abundant documents prove that the Anglo-Saxons found traces of Christianity throughout the land. No Statute Law, forming or creating Parishes, can be traced in the laws of England during any period. But many enactments can be quoted, as referring to them as established, and *confirming* them. The Saxon records note Tithe-charges as esteemed to be God's tenth among British Christians. *Palgrave,* in his Anglo-Saxon Common-wealth, referring to an enactment of Ethelwulf's time (A.D. 854), supposed to be the legislative enactment by which the lands were first subjected to the payment of tythes to the clergy, argues rather that this enactment proved that the *right of the Church* to tythes had *already been recognized* in the most unequivocal manner (vol. i. 159). Theodore, Archbishop of Canterbury (A.D. 680), tempted landed proprietors, as Justinian had done in the East, to build and endow Churches, securing to them the perpetual patronage; and in A.D. 928, the rank of *thane* was allowed to founders of Churches, in the reign of Athelstan—his was the silver penny found in the Roman Villa—one of the most able and energetic of Saxon monarchs. In 1008, Ethelred held a legislative assembly at Eanham (Ensham, Oxfordshire), when the Archbishops of Canterbury and York took the opportunity to have a large gathering, on

E 2

whom they urged the duty of building Churches in all parts of the country.

How excellent the theory; how beneficial in practice, is the Parochial system, which gives a Church, and secures the services of a Minister for *all* the people within certain limits. Pastor and people, with a mutual responsibility, looking to each other, as of right, for mutual aid; we escape the evils of mere favouritism, accompanied often by neglect of needy souls; which are evils inseparable from a mere congregational system. We gather from a multitude of proofs that our Parochial Churches, with their endowments, are *not national* foundations, but the gradual fruits of individual liberality. As each landed proprietor, when he built a Church, endowed it out of the Tithes or Land of his Estate; we have accounted for the singular discrepancy in size, and the irregularity of boundaries of Parishes. Thus the HAMLET of Wallington—once a Royal Estate—is a narrow strip of land, on the West side of Beddington Parish, having on its East, Carshalton, the "Aultone" (Old Town) of Domesday Survey. To one who had distinguished himself at the battle of Hastings as Geoffrey de Magnaville, the King would be likely to grant something worth having, as the Estate of the Old Town, &c. On the other side there must be something good for Richard de Tonbridge—his own half-brother—and Milo Crispin; both influential and distinguished characters; so there would be left to the King the land adjoining the old Town of *Saxon Waletone.* With it there would be retained some meadow land by the Wandle and the two mills. And so the Royal Manor would contain only 823 acres, stretching in a narrow strip from Beddington Corner (Mitcham

Common), beyond Woodcote, nearly three miles long; while Beddington would contain 3951 acres; and Carshalton 2926 acres.

Of the endowments of the Church of England remaining to this day, there are calculated to belong to

Pre-reformation times ..	.. £1,949,204	
Post-reformation times ..	.. £2,251,051	
		£4,200,255

From this deduct for Clerical Taxation
by c. 106 of 1 and 2 Vict. ..   714,043

£3,486,212

If the sum of these endowments were equally divided among the Clergy of the Church of England, it would give each about £201 per annum. If the sum were divided among the whole community of Church people, it would be about 6¾s. each.

It requires very little consideration to discover that the above sums are very far from a tenth (tythe) of the produce of the land of England and Wales—much less, if tithe of trade (by law of Edward the Confessor) is reckoned—and if, as some would argue, *provision for the poor* is to be taken out of these sums, it would be easy to show, if so unsound an argument needed to be met, that, actually in the present day, a good fourth of the Church's income is paid to the support of the poor. Church-rates may be traced to the special legislation of Ina, King of the West Saxons, A.D. 693; and it was, after they had been maintained as the law of the land for nearly 1200 years, that they were abrogated. Poor-rates date from 27th Henry VIII., 1536, though it was not till 1601 that the system was matured.

We have observed that there was no Church mentioned
in Domesday for the Royal Manor of Wallington. So there
was no Church in the Royal Manor of *Reigate;* though its
Saxon name in Domesday is Cherchefeld (*Church-field*),
situated on the Rige-gate, or *road*-on-the-Ridge. In course
of time it retained only the latter name—now Reigate. So
in the case of *Mortlake—the Archbishop's Manor!* Lysons
has clearly shown that there was no Church, but at Wimbledon; the Manor including Putney, as well as Wimbledon
and Mortlake. So no Church at Mitcham, held by the
Bishops and Canons of Baieux; nor at Morden, held by the
Abbey of St. Peter's, Westminster.

We should, perhaps, recall at this point that the Domesday
Survey, if accurate in facts mentioned, was not exhaustive
of all information that might then have been obtained.
Its object being to secure a correct Taxation, matters which
did not bear on this object, were passed by lightly. So
the endowments of the Church at that period are very far
from being fully stated. The counties of Northumberland,
Cumberland, Westmoreland and Durham, are not described
in the Survey. It is supposed that it was impossible to
take any exact survey of these counties, as they had suffered
so much from the Conqueror's revenge. Under the title,
" Terra regis," and land which had belonged to the Earls
Edwin and Morcar, *wasta* occurs almost everywhere.

Then in other localities, we may be sure, the iron hand
of the Norman also carried destruction; and we may well
believe there were numerous *wasta* on a smaller scale. It is
likely that the frequent contests all over our neighbourhood
through several centuries preceding the eleventh, had left
little for the Norman to destroy. No wonder if the old

Town could not survive such repeated passages of arms. Its very name, as given by Ptolemy, implies that it occupied no strong position on the Surrey Hills. " *Maes*, or more properly *magh*, signifies *field* or *plain*—as in Sitomagus, Cæsaromagus, Noviomagus." (Lower.) No wonder then that the Old Town on the Hill-plateau should fall into decay. And the *Church?* if an old British edifice? On the very spot the *wood and the clay* (at Woodcote) would supply materials for walls of *wattled work* to be plastered with the clay—as usual. If an early Saxon edifice, built of wood, like Benedict's Monastery at Monk-Wearmouth, or Green-stead Church, near Ongar, Essex, it would fall an easy prey to the flames of an enemy. Only a building of later Saxon style, copying the Norman style, would supply a solid mass of masonry that might withstand the ravages of enemies and ages. Nor is it unworthy of notice, that the shallow foundations required with the solid chalk close underneath them, would leave continually exposed to ravages of time and enemies, what would be hidden on softer land; so, few traces of the old Town are found. Thus the old Church gone, and the population of Waletone sorely diminished in Norman days—with no resident Lord of the Manor—the provision made in *Bedintone* Church must needs suffice; and the Tithes of Waleton would help to enrich Bedintone-cum-Waletone.

Again. The idea that there was a special provision for the Parson of the old Church in Wallington, arises out of the circumstance that there was a Portionist (Clergyman) who had a *large share of the Beddintone endowment.* (" 4th part;" Manning i. 93.) In A.D. 1309, there was an Episcopal commission to enquire into that case; and the return gave

that it had existed thus "ab antiquo, libera absque cura"
—from olden time free and a sinecure. Very suspicious is
this return! Nothing indeed is mentioned about Wallington
and its ruined Church. But how this *"sinecure?" from*
"olden time?" Its emoluments in 1473 (estimated at 40s.
nett) principally arose from the Tithes of 200 acres of land,
called Huscarle's Feod (fee), on the North side of the Church,
and from a house and twenty acres of land on the South
side. But in the King's books, 1533, it is valued at
£8 12s. 1d.; Beddington Rectory is £13 6s. 8d. Again:
the patronage was annexed to the Manor of Beddington
Huscarle. The old Church of Beddington was annexed to
the other Manor. All this is puzzling in the extreme. One
Portionist felt it a burden on his conscience to receive an
income, and do nothing for it. So William de Carru, on
1st March, 1342, had a license for a private Chapel in his
house in this parish. Certainly we cannot identify the
Parson of Wallington with the provision made in the will
of Carew, who died 1391, for "one Chaplain to pray for his
soul." The date would suffice to contradict this; and it
was to be *in* Beddington Church.

But still returns the question, what was the meaning of
the old building described by Lysous, and pulled down in
1791? If there was no Saxon Thane to build, some later
Lord of the Manor, seeing his people increase around him,
would, out of very love to God, and care for the souls of
his dependents, have erected such a building; not very-
early in its style—probably the 14th century? And this
was a century marked, in the annals of our neighbourhood,
by similar events. In 1342, Wm. de Carru had his Chapel
in Beddington. In 1347, Reginald le Forester had an

oratory licensed in his House, at Bandon   And in 1348,
the Huscarles had a similar license for their house at
Beddington; and Beddington Church re-built about 1390.

Was there no moving cause for this outburst of zeal?
Was it that 1348 was the year of a great Pestilence?   A
succession of earthquakes convulsed Europe; and although
England escaped this calamity, it was deluged with incessant
rain from June to December.   In August, the plague appeared
in Dorsetshire, whence it gradually extended.   Many of its
victims expired in six hours; few lingered beyond three
days.   All the cemeteries of London were soon filled—one
alone receiving 200 bodies daily, during several weeks.
From man, the pestilence extended to the brute creation.
Excessive rains then had a very different effect to what they
have now; for, on their ceasing, a malaria would arise from
the saturated land.   Thus it would be, before a proper system
of drainage prevailed, when the rising of the " Surrey
Bourne" laid the whole of the Old Town of Croydon under
water.   We may understand how it might well deserve the
name of the " *Woewater* "—preceding, too, the plague of
1665.   But that it should have appeared also before the
" Restoration of Charles II., and again in 1688—on the eve
of the " glorious Revolution," were "singular coincidences,"
which have been very rare since.   The residents among
the Chalk Hills of Hampshire are well accustomed to their
" Lavants," in every village, on the recurrence of an ex-
cessively wet season.   To them it is only a disagreeable
washing?—" Lavant."

To return.   Our architect, looking at the description of
the old Chapel, would give " 1380 *about the date.*"   Had
we any great Lord of the Manor about that time?   And

we fix upon the Lodelaws. Catharine, widow of Thomas
Lodelawe, died siesed of this Manor, A.D. 1394. That there
was a house of some considerable importance is clear from
the remains of a vaulted chamber, which still remains as
a cellar to the present Manor House. We give a *faithful*
woodcut on the opposite page.

The dimensions give a room, 28 feet in its length from
E. to W ; 15 feet wide from N. to S. ; 9 feet high to the
crown of the vaulted roof. The walls are of chalk ; the
roof is of neatly squared chalk, and is strengthened by five
massive ribs of stone, which, like the roof, are slightly
arched and pointed. Access from the the present house is
in the N.W. corner, where is a small square window and
doorway, slightly projecting, of same date as the rest of the
structure ; and in the W. wall is a square aumbrey—*locker*.
On the S. side is a more pretentious entrance, in a semi-
octagonal projection, enclosing a spiral staircase of stone,
perfect to a certain extent, but blocked up at about the
height of the roof. Here, the doorway-arch is cut out of
two large blocks of stone. The stone used is similar to
that found at Godstone—to which, it will be remembered,
there was an old road from hence direct—a stone which is
generally used in the ancient buildings of the District
(which has therefore been used by Mr. Tritton in his restoration of the Carew Chapel). The structure resembles the
style of two "Crypts" at Guildford, supposed by Brayley to
be of 14th century date. However, Mr. Brock gives this
as the domestic architecture *of the 14th century*, or *later;*
when Lodelaws and Dymocks held their "Manor Courts" at
Wallington, to which came their tenants as far as from
Kingston. This ancient vaulted chamber would form a

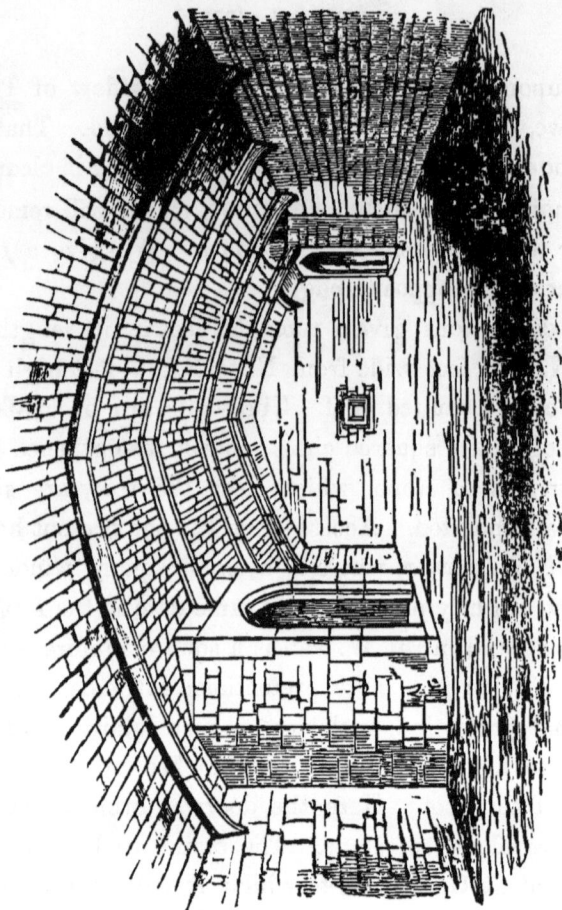

part of their Manor House; for what purpose is not clear.
That Manor House was on the site of one older still.
ROMAN bricks, built into the walls, testify. Is it much to
presume that the old Church was built by one of these
Lodelaws, or Dymocks? the Church first in point of time,
the Manor House afterwards; the *Rector of Beddington-cum-
Wallington* taking his share of the duty; and, in consideration of the tithes he received from the West of his parish,
maintaining the proper services in this Chapel of Ease?
So long as this family continued to hold the Manor, the
Church was kept up. But when the Manor fell to the
Carew family, they would feel interested mainly in Beddington; and the landed proprietor failing in his duty, it would
not be surprising if the Rector failed also; and soon all
would fall to decay, where there was no "considering one
another to provoke unto good works." And so the old
Church came down in 1791.

A record in the Beddington "Church Book" affords an
example of a "singular coincidence." How came this stir
at that particular time?

1791.

10th June—Mops, Brooms and Brushes for Church			£0	8	9
10th „	Women, for Cleaning ..	..	0	8	0
18th „	Glover's bill, for Smith's work	..	5	3	0
23rd „	Beer for Workmen and Women	..	0	15	4
22nd July—Beer for Carpenter whilst putting up Pulpit Stairs ..	..	.. ..	0	1	0

The work, too, must be hurried! and so the Saxon stimulant
was provided, in the form of BEER. "Nam tua res agitur,
paries cum proximus ardet." (Hor. Ep. 1. 18.) "For your
own affairs are in question, when your neighbour's wall is
on fire."

But Church-restoration in Wallington slept a while. Mr. Brook Allen Bridges (of whom there is a portrait, as well as of his grandfather, the Rev. N. Bridges, Rector of Wadenhoe, and his wife Sarah — Sawyer), succeeded Mr. Wm. Bridges. He was the friend of Hervey and Fletcher, Cecil and Romaine, Newton and Wilberforce; and identified with every good work connected with that blessed revival of religion, which took place in the Church of England at the beginning of this century. He died in 1815, and was suceeded by his brother John; during whose time the Mansion was generally let—notably, to the late Lord Chief Justice Denman. At his death, in 1833, his son John succeeded. The Collector of these "Notes" well remembers a profitable week spent in his company and that of his brother Charles (the well-known author of a Commentary on Psalm cxix., and other works), during a tour in the West of England, on behalf of the Church Missionary Society. There was, at that time, much discussion on the subject of Elementary Education. Mr. Kay Shuttleworth's wise plans for providing a suitable supply of Teachers had lately come into operation. In view of these plans, the Wallington School of that day would be discussed; the Pestalozzian system; the Home and Colonial School, in Gray's Inn Road; and the Mayos, brother and sister. But there was little thought in the mind of one of the party, how deep an interest the locality would assume for him; when, in God's Providence, the Wallington School would become his charge. Then its history unfolded itself.

Iu 1833—when Mr. Bridges inherited the property—in consultation wilh the Misses Wallace and Mr. Robt. Loraine, what plan would be most beneficial to the neighbourhood, it was decided to commence a Girls' School. Mr. R.

Loraine, now 47 years ago, had opened a Boys' School, at fourpence for each scholar per week, under Mr. Price. It was held in the house, which is ·opposite "the *Pump*"— *Oxdon Place* is the other side of the road. During sixteen years, the average attendance was about seventy boys. There was a Sunday-School—130 boys, oftentimes, clothed at Mr. Loraine's expense. To carry out the plan of a Girls' School, Mr. Bridges threw two cottages into one, so giving the old *Long-room* at the present School, with the Teacher's apartments over; and Mrs. Christmas was the first Mistress. The School soon grew too large for the existing accommodation, and consequently, in 1839, a suitable room was built (which forms now a part of our School-room proper), so that Girls and Infants received, separately, the instruction needed. So matters continued till the Rev. James Hamilton came as Rector of the Parish, Beddington-cum-Wallington. He thought he saw a re-arrangement of educational affairs was needed; and with the aid of liberal subscriptions from the Parishioners generally, the present building was erected and opened in 1843, by the side of the Croydon road, for the children of Beddington and Wallington. Mr. Price was transferred from Wallington, as the Master; and Miss Cannan, of Wallington, was appointed Mistress, for the new Schools. The Wallington School was continued under Mrs. Christmas for Infants only. A School and residence was erected at Beddington Corner in 1843, in memory of the Rev. W. B. Ferrers; and in Dr. Marsh's time, a room for Infants was added at the Beddington School. Many an old scholar retains a lively and grateful remembrance of the instruction received under these arrangements.

School matters continued in Wallington nnchanged, till increasing infirmities necessitated the resignation of Mrs. Christmas, after 31½ years' service. It was then decided to place the School under Government inspection, thus securing an unprejudiced opinion on the state of the School, annually; and also, proportionately to its real efficiency, obtaining pecuniary aid. Miss Burnand was accordingly appointed Mistress in March, 1838, and the School was re-organized, for Infants and older children, to meet the needs the new Parish of Holy Trinity; and soon it was apparent that more accommodation was needed.

Nor were the requisite funds lacking. The enlargement was effected without any extraneous aid from any Public Fund, at a cost of £237, in the summer of 1870. Though the Council of Education requirements expect, generally, provision to be made in Elementary Schools for one-sixth of the population; yet ours suffices for our particular case— supplying accommodation for 116 children, 8 square feet to each, or sitting room for an adult audience of 200. The premises are well used in educational work. Mothers' meetings; an Evening School; a Science School, noted for its success in teaching Drawing for Mechanics, &c.; Choral Societies; Evening Lectures, and Entertainments of every variety, can testify.

And the Daily School flourishes. Miss Burnand having been compelled by ill-health to resign, to the general regret of those interested, Miss Hallaway has succeeded to the charge; and the population of the neighbourhood still supplies its quota of children—Girls, Boys, and Infants. The School Premises have been dedicated by the Lord of the Manor, with the hearty good will of the Parishioners, for use as a School for ever, to be conducted on the *Principles of the Reformed Church of England*. Thus our School in Wallington forms one of those 19,549 Week-day Schools in England and Wales, in which are educated, by the Church, 1,187,086 children (*Newcastle Commission*). In the Educational *Blue Book* for 1870–71, there were 6,382 Church of England Schools *under inspection*, besides 1,549 Protestant Nonconformist Schools—not quite a fourth of the number of the Church of England Schools.

Church of England people have also built twenty-eight Training Colleges; in which were being trained, in 1871, 1,666 students; and provided, at least, one-fourth of the funds required for the maintenance of those Institutions.

The National Society for promoting the Education of the Poor in the principles of the Established Church, was instituted in 1811, and has expended nearly a million pounds in Educational work (more than four-fifths of which expenditure was for building Schools and Training Colleges) calling forth, at least, twelve times that amount from members of the Church of England.

But these sums of money do not include the many Schools also built throughout the country without aid from any Public Fund—as our School has been erected. We have thus a tolerable idea of the work of the Church of England in Primary Education.

We now turn from our School to our Church affairs, which had been standing still since 1791—though not uncared for, nor undiscussed. The thoughtful mind of the Rev. Jas. Hamilton had anticipated the event of another Church; and not only was it discussed by him with Mr. J. Bridges, but it was provided for in the administration of

some Parochial matters, and the status of the future
Minister legally defined. It was, therefore, to the honoured
memory of his father, and subservient to the glory of God,
that the New Church was planned by Mr. N. Bridges, at
first on a smaller scale than it now appears : but afterwards
enlarged to meet the ideas of two friends who, unsolicited,
offered aid for the work of making it a building capable of
holding 500 persons. It was carried out by Mr. Simpson,
from the designs of Mr. E. P. L. Brock; and consecrated
28th September, 1867, by the Bishop of the Diocese (*Sumner*)
under the title of " Holy Trinity Church, Wallington." It
affords seats for 530 persons (of which 150 are free seats),
and is thus adequate to a population far more than our
locality can as yet supply. And, at any rate, it should
always be more than sufficient for whatever may be the
population on Mr. N. Bridges' property, which is 73 acres
out of 522 acres.

The Architect of our Church has chosen an exterior
style, as nearly as possible, resembling the description of
the old Chapel, after the style of the middle of the 14th
century. The west window of the South Aisle is similar
to one in the Church of little St. Mary's, Cambridge, which
was erected about 1350. Each window has a tracery of a
different pattern. The stone, used with the flints, is Bath-
stone. The roof is covered with Broseley tiles, of which
description are the floor tiles also. The height of the spire
is 110 feet. The interior of the Church gives an area of
105 feet long and 51 feet broad.

The interior *arrangements* are in accordance with
primitive customs.

The East end of the Church is a distinctive feature—

technically called an octagonal Apse. Its form is of great antiquity, and appears to have been adopted by the early Christians from the plan of the Roman *Basilicas*, or *Public Halls;* many of which were turned into Churches in the Constantine period. Almost all the early Churches had an Apse—that is, the segment of a *wheel*—as the shape of their Eastern side; and there are traces of several, of Saxon date, still remaining in England; one of which, at Wing, in Bedfordshire, is polygonal on plan, and not octagonal. The Apse, octagonal, is a marked feature in most Continental Churches, even of late date; though, in England, it is rarely found after the Norman period. There remains an apse, octagonal, in the ruined Church, called the *Friary*, at Winchelsea, Sussex, erected about 1350, and nearly the same as that of Wallington Church. In the name Church we trace the Eastern origin, *Kuriakon* (*Greek* sound); and in Saxon, *Kyric*, or *Kyrck;* Scottice, Kirk—of or *belonging to the Lord*. We will go back a moment to the East—the cradle of Christianity—and take an account of Churches there in the time of *our* Constantine, then Emperor of the Roman world; when Church-building may be said to have received its first important impulse—alas! too often, afterward, in the direction of error.

Bingham's Ecclesiastical Antiquities will inform us that there was no uniform plan. We gather that the Church, generally, was of an oblong shape. The Church which Constantine built over our Saviour's sepulchre, at Mount Golgotha, was *Round*. That which he built at Antioch was an *Octagon*. The Church of the Apostles, built by Constantine, at Constantinople, was in the form of a *Cross*—not a *Latin* cross. They were commonly so placed, as that the

F

front or chief entrances were on the West side of the building, and the place for the Communion Table on the East side. But at Antioch the very reverse was the case; and at Tyre also. St. Patrick, in Ireland, built a Church that stood from North to South. In those days the Building was divided into three parts:

1. The entrance, as it were, where the penitents and catechumens stood. This part was often called the *Narthex*. (Physicians called their works on the cure of diseases, *nartheces*. The reed-stalk, in which Prometheus is fabled to have conveyed the spark of fire from heaven to earth, is so called.)

2. The *Naos*, or *temple*, where the Communicants had their places in due order.

3. The *Bema*, raised above the level of the rest—which, in the early Churches of the East, took the form of an *Apse*, or resembled a *Shell*.

Around and against the walls of the Apse were the Bishop's seat, and the seats of the Presbyters on each side, arranged in a semi-circular form. Tho place of the COMMUNION TABLE could not, therefore, be close to the wall at the upper end, but at some little distance from it, The Communion Table was made of *Wood* up to the time of Constantine, who caused some Tables to be made of *Silver*; afterwards, *Marble* was introduced; and then, with magnificence of buildings, there came in corruptions—the table became an Altar. We have no cross among our Church ornaments. In the time of Constantine there was none.

Chrysostom writes (A.D 398) of the sign of the cross, as used at the Lord's table, in the consecration of presbyters, and the celebration of the Eucharist; but that was the transient sign, made on the forehead, and not any material cross. In fact, the custom of setting up the material cross in churches is not to be traced so early as the age of Constantine. And the cross of the early Church was not at all the representation of the *Latin* Cross, on which our Lord was crucified; the Holy Spirit guarding the Infant Church against the corruptions, which only a later age witnessed. Lady Eastlake, in her continuation of Mrs. Jameson's History of our Lord, as exemplified in works of art, states, " ancient objects of art, as far as hitherto known, afford no corroboration of the use of the cross in the simple transverse form (Latin cross) familiar to us, at any period preceding, or even closely succeeding St. Chrysostom." But in another form the cross, if not actually seen, is indicated—that is, on the so-called monogram of Christ. It was in A.D. 311, on the eve of his great battle with Maxentius, which gave him the sway of the Roman world, that the supposed vision of a luminous cross appeared to this Emperor, in the sky, accompanied by the words, " In hoc signo vinces "—" In this sign thou shalt conquer." But no description exists to determine the exact form in which this supposed vision appeared. Neither is it written what species of cross it was which Constantine erected, resplendent with jewels, on the Palace at Byzantium (to be thenceforward Constantinople); nor yet has any writer sufficiently described the sacred banner, or " Labarum," which preceded his armies in all engagements; or the cross which he inscribed on the shields of his soldiers. But on the coinage of his son Constantius, who became Emperor in 353, and reigned till 361, a representation of the Labarum, or sacred banner, began to appear. And the

F 2

Labarum appears on a coin of Valentinian, in our Museum.
We have had kindly lent us, by Lady Eastlake, an illustration from a coin of that time.   Observe, the monogram—
composed of two Greek letters.   The
X, or Ch., and P, which is the Greek
R—the first consonants of the Greek
word *Christ;*   as I.H.S. are the first
letters of Jesus in Greek.   The coins
of this period are many, and various
in size; yet in no single instance does
the simple Latin cross appear.   In the
early Mosaics at Ravenna, which represent the Emperor
Justinian (A.D. 528) and the Empress Theodora, the body
guard attending them are seen with their shields inscribed,
not with the cross, but with the monogram.   By Rubens,
too, in his series of the History of Constantine, as connected
with the apparition of the Cross, the vision is represented
in the full form of the monogram.

Surely this is plain teaching—clearly proving the early
Christians looked to CHRIST, not the material cross; in fact,
avoided representations of that instrument of the death of
Christ; looking rather to Him, who hung thereon.

In the old British Church of Perranzabuloe (Cornwall),
the remains of which were unburied in 1835, "there were
no traces of rood-loft, nor latticed confessional, nor sa'cring
bell; no images, or paintings of saints, to sanction a breach
of second commandment; no censers, crucifixes, rosaries—
not one—not the remnant of one could be be discovered,
after most diligent search," though the mass of sand had
preserved much that would otherwise have perished from
exposure.   A curious old Cross stood there a few years

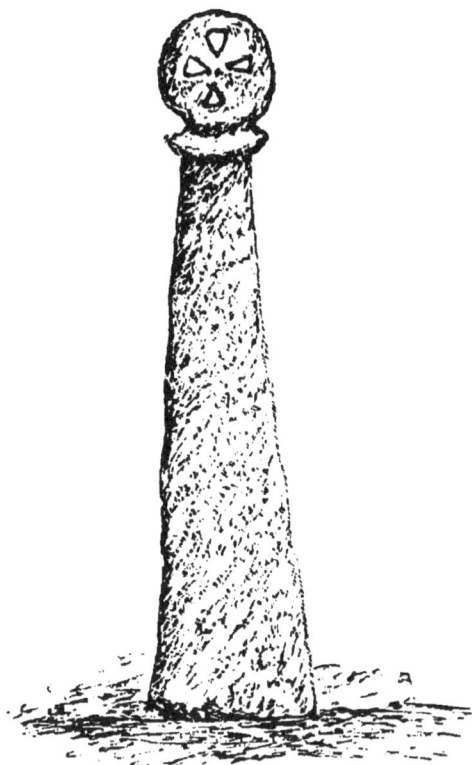

Old Cross
a/h
Perranzabuloe.

ago. It is formed after the rudest mode, by three holes which perforate, and a fourth cut only a little way into, the rounded head, of what the Cornish people denominate the "*Men Skryfd*," or "inscribed stone." It measures 13 feet in height, four of which are buried in the sand. This memorial of early Christian art, is probably as ancient as the time of Piranus, to whose memory this old Church was dedicated, being built at the beginning of the 5th century— fully a hundred years after Constantine's era—over 100 years before Augustine arrived from Rome (A.D. 597), and in form, not resembling the Latin cross. You have an illustration on the opposite side, copied by permission from "*Perranzabuloe*," by Rev. T. C. Collins. (*Rivingtons*.)

But it was in Constantine's time that the Eastern side of the Church began to be accounted more sacred than the rest; a separation beginning to be made by means of rails —*cancelli*, whence comes Chancel. The most ancient custom was for men and women to come up to the holy Table to communicate; but the council of Laodicea (A.D. 367) particularly forbids women so to do. Soon after there were veils or hangings to divide the Chancel from the rest of the building; and in England, history relates, that in some buildings, above a high Chancel screen (making, as it were, the Holy of Holies of the Jewish Temple), there was placed a massive Latin cross; or a crucifix (representing our Lord on the cross), often with sundry figures of Apostles and later Saints, which place was styled the *rood- loft—cross-loft*, we might say. At the Reformation, in the Canons of 1571, Churchwardens were charged to remove "all rood-lofts, in which wooden crosses formerly stood, and other relics of superstition." Queen Elizabeth was favourable to them; but the Reformers stood firm; and crosses continued forbidden. And as for Ornaments? the 82 Canon orders "the Ten Commandments to be set up on the East End of every Church and Chapel, where the people may best see and read the same; and other chosen sentences written upon the walls, in places convenient."

By the Liturgy of 1552, "The Table stood in the body of the Church, or in the Chancel." Laud, aided by arbitrary power, succeeded in having the Table placed, generally, "altarwise" against the East end. But as there is nothing in the New Testament, so there is nothing in our Liturgy to encourage this; where the word "altar" is not used even once.

The separation of the sexes in time of Divine Service is an Eastern idea. Chrysostom expressly records, "it was not so from the beginning." Frequently the women were confined to "galleries," as is the case in Jewish synagogues.

The Singers as well as the Readers had their places assigned them in the Ambon, which was in the Nave, rather nearer the principal entrance than the middle of the Church. In the Apostolic age "all the congregation lifted up their voice with one accord." But the Council of Laodicea forbad all others to sing in Church besides the canonical singers, who went up into the Ambon, and sung by book; and afterwards the singers were withdrawn into the Chancel, which was also called the Chorus—whence Choir. Music is as ancient as the Apostles—but not instrumental music. The use of Organs in Churches came into the Church since the time of Thomas Aquinas, A.D. 1250. The instrument is much more ancient, but not in Church-service. Doubtless there were no Messrs. Walker to supply seraphic sounds;

else, surely, they would have had one of their instruments to assist the Choir; as we now have (December, 1872), and doubtless they would have paid all the money for it, *as we hope to do ere long.*

Then as for Bells? For the first three hundred years, they did not have even one, as we have, the gift of our honoured friend, Lord Fitzwalter, from the foundry of Messrs. Mears. Who brought bells first into use for calling the faithful to prayer, is a thing yet undetermined. But no date earlier than the seventh century can be named. Paulinus, Bishop of Nola, in Campania, is said to have introduced them; but in describing his Church, which he does very minutely, he takes no notice of Tower or Bells. Hentzer (a German, visiting England in 1598) gives a curious account of English customs, and describes minutely Nonsuch Palace in Elizabeth's day, and has given drawings of it, and the Queen's equipages. He writes: "The English are vastly fond of great noises that fill the ear; such as firing of cannon, beating of drums, and ringing of bells. It is common among the people, for a number of them, that have got a glass in their heads, to get up into some belfry, and ring the bells for hours together, for the sake of exercise!" We, of Wallington, have a floor ready to receive the peal; only we hope their vibration will not interfere with the CLOCK, for which are windows ready in our Tower. Our Architect has given us a handsome SPIRE, but no WEATHERCOCK! We cannot say whether this arose from unwillingness to perpetuate the memory of Peter's denial of our Lord; or that he wished us to understand that we ought "not to be carried about with every wind of doctrine," but should keep firm in our Church to "the faith once for all delivered to the saints."

Yet one, not primitive, fashion we have in our Church at Wallington—the Baptismal Font *inside* the Church. Up to the sixth age, the Baptisteries were *outside the Church.* But we can lay no great stress on that, before Him who "will have mercy, not sacrifice." Many a mother rejoices to think that the prayers of the congregation go forth for her child within the Church; and the most tender or scrupulous parent may be satisfied that the babe may be "sprinkled" only with the water; or "dipped" in the water, as our font is sufficiently large to allow it.

The characteristics of our Church will thus be sufficiently explained. Its completion and consecration witnessed the commencement of the Parsonage adjoining, which was completed by July of 1868, at the expense mainly of Mr. N. Bridges, with the aid of the Ecclesiastical Commissioners, who added an endowment of £33 per annum. A separate District has been assigned by an Order of the Queen in Council, in December, 1867; and, since under the Blandford Act, it has become the New Parish of Holy Trinity, Wallington, comprehending all that portion of the Hamlet, to the south of a line drawn across from E. to W., including "My Garden."

We now turn to Beddington. You have a view of the Carew Mansion and the old Church as they appeared "one hundred years ago." During the incumbency of the Rev. J. B. Ferrers, in 1829, the Church Tower was partly rebuilt. In 1839, a new Organ was erected after the whole edifice had undergone a thorough overhauling. But in 1850, when the Rev. Jas. Hamilton was Rector, it was

discovered that the roof was in a dangerous state; and a new roof was scarcely in its place, when it was found that pillars on the north side were giving way. " For a moment it was thought that the old Church must come down. But the parishioners stood forward. The Churchwardens (Mr. Engström and Mr. Juggins) showed a noble zeal; and sufficient funds were soon obtained, not only to set right the roof and pillars, but to add an entire new Aisle (the North) and substitute oak sittings for the close and cumbrous pews. The Rector and his friends restored the Chancel; and stained glass windows were contributed, so that it was supposed to be 'one of the most attractive Churches in Surrey.' "

But all this was as nothing compared with the work commenced in 1869 by Rev. A. H. Bridges, aided by his friends. We cannot enumerate all the "extensive and costly additions," so we will endeavour to summarize from the account in *The Church Builder*, No. xxxii.

" A new organ chamber on the N. side of the Chancel, with Organ by Lewis; richly carved oak organ screen, by Morris; windows of organ chamber, painted glass by Lavers and Co.

" The Chancel restored—new reredos, in mosaics—sides of E. window marble mosaics—retable, sedilia, piscina, replaced. Sacrarium laid in English and foreign marbles and serpentine. Stalls and misereres; choir seats—all in oak. New oak chancel-screen. Iron corona and pendants, by Skidmore. Altar candlesticks, by Hart. Nave, aisles, porch and seating, thoroughly restored; carvings improved in character. Walls decorated in diaper, slightly coloured, by Bell and Co. Fresco (?) of imposing character and beauty at W. end of N. aisle. Windows filled with painted glass, by Clayton. Old organ and gallery removed. Inside of tower restored; a peal of ten bells, by Mears. Exterior stone work restored; roofs covered with lead. A new vestry, with singing room over—somewhat of a secular character; windows all filled with painted glass. Ground outside Church lowered, levelled, drained. A new entrance on W. side. Lych gate, resembling one at Beckenham. The whole of the work done from and under the directions of the Architect, Mr. Jos. Clarke."

In " Brayley's Surrey " we are told, " The following particulars respecting the Charities in this parish are inscribed on the front of the Organ gallery :—

" *Donations and bequests to the Parish of Beddington and Wallington.*

"Dec. 5th, 1825. Mrs. Ann Paston Gee bequeathed, by her will, £,1000, to be invested in the Funds; the interest thereof to be given to the Poor on Christmas Eve, in every year.

" 1625. Henry Smith, by will, bequeathed £2 per year, to the poor of Beddington.

" Feb. 6th, 1830. John Bristow, Esq., £100 interest.

" Several allotments of land were awarded by the Commissioners under the Inclosure Act (52nd Geo. III. c. 208) for the use of the poor. They also awarded a piece of land, called 'Church Mead,' to Beddington Church, 1 acre and 29 perches.

" Mrs. Ann Paston Gee gave a piece of land called ' Cat's brains,' containing 3 acres and 5 perches, in exchange for cottages and land on Chat's Hill, also belonging to Beddington Church.

"William Bridges, Esq., gave £200, 3 per cent. Consolidated Bank Annuities (it should be 3 per cent. Consols) to the poor of the Hamlet of Wallington, on account of the enclosure of a piece of land in the same Hamlet."

To this we may add the gift of Mrs. Martha *Medland* (who lived in the Cayley family, once occupants of Elm Grove), " £43 14s. 9d. Bank Stock, for an annual donation of coals to the poor of Wallington, at Christmas."

The Carew Chapel, on S. side of Chancel, was built about 1520, and the "founder's tomb" placed there. Such chapels were frequently erected and used as burial places, when the idea prevailed that there was a peculiar efficacy in burials within a consecrated building. The Romans wisely buried away from the haunts of men. And, in our day, more wholesome regulations prevail; and our sanitary laws forbid burials in Churches. The present proprietor (Mr. H. Tritton) has adapted it for worship; and it has been faithfully restored, unaltered, under the able superintendence of Mr. W. Butterfield.

Turning to the Carew Mansion, Sir Francis built the magnificent House in which he had the honor of entertaining Queen Elizabeth twice—18th Aug., 1599, and 16th Aug., 1600. About the year 1709, Sir Nicholas Carew rebuilt the Mansion on a grand scale—forming three sides of a square. The interior of the North wing was destroyed by fire shortly after it was finished, and it was never restored by the Carews. The *Manor* House, adjoining the Church, is thoroughly suggestive of the origin of Churches and Parishes; as already explained. When the last of the Carew property was sold, the Mansion, with land and gardens adjoining, was purchased for the *Lambeth Female*

Orphan Asylum, and the whole building underwent a thorough renovation. Of the old Mansion, 1528, only the Hall remains still—an admirable specimen of the Domestic architecture of the period; and a curious old Lock is still to be seen. But the famed orange grove is gone—as from Carshalton, at Sir W. Scawen's. The last of the name who died was not connected with this ancient family. Richard Gee, Esq., of Orpington, Kent, was the grandson of Philippa, sister of Sir Fras. Carew (who died in 1689) and inherited Beddington under the will of Sir N. Hacket Carew, who died in 1762. He assumed, under authority of an Act of Parliament, the name and arms of Carew. That gentleman, dying unmarried in 1816, demised all his property to the widow of his brother William, who had been resident at Beddington, and died there in 1815. Mrs. Gee died in 1828, and bequeathed her property to her first cousin—. Admiral Sir Benjm. Hallowell, G.C.B., Nelson's companion in arms, and a hero of the Nile. Pursuant to the will of his relative, he assumed, by royal license, the name and arms of Carew. On his decease, he was succeeded by his eldest son in 1834. It was his grandson, Chas. Hallowell Carew, who died and was buried at Beddington last year.

Now that we are at Beddington we will first take our survey there with the aid of the very oldest inhabitants, and then return home to Wallington. We are at the Church and the *Great House*, as it was then called; or *Beddington Park*. To drive there, our carriage must have turned to the left, opposite the entrance gates of the present Rectory, built during the incumbency of the Rev. Jas. Hamilton, in 1844; and, on the right hand, we should have passed a house, famous in Beddington story, as supposed to be the house in which *the Portionist* lived; afterwards occupied by succeeding Rectors of Beddington for nearly 200 years, till they very excusably fancied it was their own Rectory House. But a law suit decided otherwise, and the Carews obtained possession of it. Query? How did the Carews come to swallow up this "house and twenty acres of land?" (see p. 55). However, Mr. Tritton rented this house from the Carews, and resided there. It has since been taken down; and the old road exchanged for the present. And now we must leave our carriage at the Church gates, as, to see the Village properly, we must walk; and we pass along the wall that encloses the gardens of the old Mansion, till we come to a gateway; in which an old entrance is restored by the proprietor, Mr. H. Tritton, whose care is seen on your right, in the preservation of the grand old Elm Trees, on each side of a path that leads out to the road. Cross the road; turn up the pretty path on the left; you have on the right, Queenswood (Mr. Norman Watney's residence). On the crown of the hill is the entrance to what has the sanction of long usage for its name, of Queen Elizabeth's Walk, or the "Ladye Walk." There were old trees there, too—as old as the days when she honoured Beddington with a visit. She is reported as having visited this spot, surrounded by her gay Court. And almost as gay, oftentimes, that walk appeared in the memory of some of our old friends, "when George the Third was King." Then it was the resort of the grand people in the neighbourhood after their early dinner hour. The ladies would come "in a dress like a Dresden Shepherdess, with high-heeled shoes, followed by a pug-dog with his tightly curled tail, or, mayhap, a lapdog in arms.

Then the beaux—possibly a plum-coloured coat, white silk stockings with pink clocks, pink silk breeches, and pink satin waistcoat." Such a description surely describes the "pink of perfection," if we add hair-powder, and a long queue! Yet it was a pleasant stroll on the rising ground, from whence a tolerably distant view may be had of the country round, with the air fresh off the Downs. And occasionally would draw up a carriage and four, with postillions and outriders in scarlet, with my Lord Derby's family from the "Oaks;" or some other equipage of the neighbourhood; and after *quantum suff.* of chat, there would be an adjournment to "the Great House," or some other in the Village, for tea, etc.

But the old trees were cut down in 1835. Miss Ferrers has kindly favoured us with some original lines, written at the time, by Miss Charlotte Cookson:—

TO THE MEMORY OF THE LADYE WALK, BEDDINGTON.

[Written in A.D. 1835, by MISS CHARLOTTE COOKSON.]

The Village pleads in vain—the doom is past,
And thou, sweet Grove, art sacrificed at last.
Thy graceful line of variegated shade,
That crowned the summit of the far-spread glade,
O'er which the sun of centuries has been shed,
And countless moons their silvery lustre spread,
O'er which the storms of ages rushed in vain,
Destroying man has levelled to the plain.
No vestige left to tell our sons, that hero
Rose the green bowr's to their forefathers dear.
The Village Pride!—a haunt beloved by all,
By every rank regretted in its fall—

Dear to the cultured mind, that loves to trace
In thought, the footsteps of an ancient race.
And to the rustic heart, who views thy shade,
Dear by a thousand recollections made.

Oft have I seen, between thy parted maze,
The hoary peasant stand awhile to gaze,
Where glows beneath the summer evening's sun
The cultured fields, where youthful work was done;
His hands, for toil or mischief powerless now,
Crossed on his staff—while he rememembers how
His happy childhood shouted in the breeze,
Plunged in the tangled brake, or climbed the trees.
Again—in youth or manhood's graceful pride
He courted here, his mistress and his bride.
Advancing still in years—this path they trace,
On Sabbath eve, with all their infant race.
Ev'n now, though haply in the world alone,
He loves the spot which these delights have known.
A Royal footstep, and a Royal name
Hallowed thy shade, and gave it half its fame.
Her feet, to which the Powers of Europe bowed,
Prest this lone path, and left the courtly crowd.
That regal eye, that quelled the pride of men,
Glanced kind approval o'er thy quiet glen;
That lofty mind, that bore resistless sway,
And made her people from the heart obey;
That in their love, with pious energy
From superstition set our altars free,
Mused in this green retreat—awhile alone,
And wished, perchance, its quiet were her own.

Alas! alas! this innovating age!
Nor Bower, nor Altar can withstand its rage.
How oft we see the purest gift of Heaven,
These little pleasures by our Maker given
To soothe our labours—raise our grateful trust,

Ourselves destroy and trample in the dust.
And can it be? The saddened thoughts that rise,
As from this ruined scene I cast my eyes
To where arises from the neighbouring plain
The loved, the venerated village Fane;
Is there an omen in these fallen trees,
Of future changes, yet more sad than these?
When, haply like these prostrate elms, be laid
The Faith established by that Royal Maid.
And in the *liberal* (?) maxims of the day,
Our simple, ancient worship melt away.
There is a Power that can avert the blow,
If we, His creatures, our obedience know.
There is a Power that can our light remove
In due chastisement of our want of love.

Farewell, sweet grove! altho' thy shade no more
Speaks to the heart of pleasant days of yore;
Although no more thy noble boughs on high
Wave over man their shadowy canopy;
And shelter from the sunlight's dazzling power
In thy lone path, his meditative hour;
Though there no more the feather'd warblers range,
May Nature aid thee to resist the change;
Reft of thy leaves, and prostrate on the plain
Still may thy spirit in the earth remain:
Thy roots retain their birthright in the soil,
And mock the spade and ploughshare's useless toil,
Mindful of former honours—wild and free
Indignant scorn a vulgar field to be;
And upward send a never-ceasing race
Of springing saplings to supply thy place;   •
The long grass there in greenest native hue
Harbour the primrose and the violet blue.
And village children to thy brakes resort
To pluck wild roses for their May-day sport;
And wandering lovers on their moonlight way
Shall pause, regretful on thy bounds, and say
(While sad remembrance checks their social talk)
" That Copsewood fringe was once our LADYE WALK."

But we have left Her Majesty in the Great House. We pass on up Church Street; and we stand on the brow of "Chat's Hill." What a curious name! But 15th Sept., 1854, there was an exchange between Mrs. Gee and the Parish, of a piece of land and five cottages on "Chat's Hill" for "Cat's-brains!"—a name of more than one piece of land hereabout. Besides, we have "Goose Green," and "Smoke shot." However, we are on the brow of Chat's Hill, and we stand to admire that old House—where the Post Office is. What a pretty sketch last year a Croydon artist made of it! It is sometimes called the "Manor House;" on what ground we cannot tell.

We turn round and mark the magnificent Cedar in front of "Brandries House"—then occupied by Sir Francis Baring—now by Mr. Joseph Laurence. On W. side of road, opposite, was the old Workhouse. And whence that old name "Brandries?" "I cannot tell," quoth our old friend, "unless it has something to do with 'Brandy-bottle Hill,' after you have passed Mr. Lambert's snuff mill, on the road to Croydon." And then we remembered what our old friend knew nothing of—that Camden writes of "Beddington:" "At some distance from hence is *Bottle-Hill*, on the top of which is a Roman Camp, with a single rampart, and square; and another on the top of a neighbouring hill, near Katerham." And our friend, Mr. West, wanted to persuade us that the site of Mr. Laurence's house is the site of an old Camp! But enough of Roman antiquities, our readers will say. We answer, "make a note of it." Continuing our walk by "Wandle side," the road on the right hand is called "Hillier's:" (?) in memory of him who coined a Beddington halfpenny in the 17th century.

G

The house now occupied by Mr. H. Tritton, was then
occupied by the family of Walton. The Bristow family
also are to be noted; and the house, where Rev. A. H.
Bridges now lives, was occupied by the Wests. It was
then called "the Manor House." Whence this name?
Was it the House of the old Huscarle Manor? We think
not. Inasmuch as *Huscarle's feod* was *on the North side of
the Church;* we are inclined to suppose the rest of that
property was situated thereabouts—if not identical with the
land, in olden time, the property of him, who possessed the
Roman Villa. The house now occupied by Mr. Shaw, the
property of the Piggott family, is on the site (?) very
nearly of the Huscarle Manor House—on *the Craneford
river,* where the Prior of St. Mary Overy had some land;
and from whence he derived a pleasing tribute of trout;
which the same river rendered also to our friend in his boy
days. Then "the Manor House" was the residence of the
Foresters? who one time held the Manor of Bandon.

But who shall unravel all these antiquarian labyrinths?
The papers of the Carew and many other families might
have helped. But the old documents are not; worthless to
any one, except the antiquarian. There was no Mr.
Oldbuck to look after them. However, we have a tale to
tell about that very locality where we now are. "My
Garden" mentions, "in the grounds of Mr. Watney, a cave,
of which many *fabulous* tales are told;" "continued to
Reigate!" &c. Here is a *true tale.* One of my old friends
informed me that it was at one time largely used in de-
frauding the officers of Her Majesty's customs. When it
became too notorious, a move was made to safer quarters.
It was one blustering night, at the beginning of this

century, that a traveller arrived at the " Plough "—a weary horse and heavily-laden panniers. Could he get on to Barrow-hedges ?—then a roadside alehouse, of not over good repute with the Excise officers. Mine host of the " Plough," with obliging readiness, soon found the traveller a guide, and forth the traveller set—labouring through the deep sloughs of Beddington. " Oh ! sir, it was a bad road then ; and opposite to where the School now is, it *was bad.*" But the guide plodded on steadily, with lantern in hand, ever and anon carefully warning and lighting the traveller past some slough, deeper than another, till they arrived safely at the " Barrow-hedges Inn." The traveller would fain reward his guide liberally for his trudge that stormy night. " Can'st not see, man ?" he exclaimed, as he held out the coin, which the guide did not take. " Why, sir, it be Dick Simpson ! and he be blind !" Dick Simpson was the man who stood to mind the gate across the road at the corner of what is now *Mr. Mackenzie's* garden wall, in Wallington. All the country round knew him well; but a stranger did not.

We are back again in Wallington—at home. " Our Village " then was concentrated, as you might expect, in the neighbourhood of the Manor House. An attempt had been made to convert it into a manufacturing village. Mr. Kilburn had set up extensive cotton-print works ; and Mr. Reynolds had set up at Hackbridge " a manufactory for the bleaching of linens, the most extensive in the kingdom. Two hundred acres of meadow land are frequently covered with cloth, mostly of Russia and Irish fabrick. Mr. Foster Reynolds, in 1786, purchased this property, and built a house on an elevated part of it." (Manning). And at the

G 2

close of the last century, and beginning of this, bleaching grounds extended all over the lands in Wallington, on the left side of the Manor Road, up to where our Church now stands. It was common land, uninclosed then. The inclosure award dates from 1853, only.

Mr. Manico's *Paper* Mill was built by Mr. Kilburn for Print works. "My Garden" was a bleaching-ground, in which stood a small Factory, built by *Mr. Grubb.* How thoroughly the name anticipated the future destinies of that land under the active supervision that has carried out "My Garden." The road passed through two streams, one running across "My Garden." These required two foot-bridges. The present Bridge was built in 1812. The house in which Mr. Purser resides was built by Mr. Newton; afterwards occupied by the Barwell Brown family.

People had some idea that our neighbourhood was a prosperous locality. The Beddington Church Book makes it appear, in those days, as if there was little difference between Beddington and Wallington; the *Church Book* making the rate, as for instance, £105 and £103 respectively, and frequently in similar proportions.

Hence, in 1801, an Act of Parliament was passed for making an "IRON RAILWAY" from Wandsworth to Croydon, with a branch to Carshalton (Hackbridge). This was not for a Railroad *Steam Locomotive.* The first of this description was introduced by Mr. Trevethick, at Merthyr, in 1804. Stephenson's improved locomotive was first made for the Killingworth Colliery in 1813. Our branch of the L. B. and S. C. RAILWAY was opened in 1844. An iron tramway had been made in 1767, at Coalbrook Dale. Doubtless the railway idea was encouraged by the busy little river Wandle "turning nearly forty mills of different kinds in its course of scarcely ten miles." (Brayley.) Who can say water-power will not have its value again, with *dear coals?* And the Population ?

	Houses.				Population		Occupation.		
	Inhabited.	Families.	Building.	Empty.	Females.	Total.	Families in Agriculture	Trade and Manufacture	Other classes.
1811—Carshalton ..	269	323	4	8	786	1532	107	147	69
Beddington ..	74	74	—	1	216	446	44	16	14
Wallington ..	134	177	1	—	409	804	44	101	32
1871—Carshalton ..	733	—	50	104	1853	3657	—	—	—
Beddington ..	257	—	27	—	824	1510	—	—	—
Wallington N.	80	86	—	6	253	497	—	—	—
Holy Trinity Parish	159	170	46	34	491	853	—	—	—

We may add that the gross Valuation of Beddington was, last year, £17,844, 19s. 6d.; the rateable value being £15,303 13s. The gross value of the Hamlet of Wallington was £14,576 11s.; the rateable value of Holy Trinity Parish being £9,950; and of the North portion of the Hamlet, £2,177.

We thus gather a little how the world has progressed in our neighbourhood. But of Manufactures? In our Parish there is only Mr. Manico's Paper Mill, employing scarcely a score hands. To the North of our Parish, in the Hamlet, there is Messrs. Frost's Skin-factory. The old Flock Mill is untenanted; and at Beddington Corner is a Flour Mill, and Messrs. Aitken's Drug Mill, and Messrs. McCrae's Tanning establishment—which last is really in Carshalton Parish.

So we turn back on the memories of the past; in the young days of our oldest inhabitants. There was then Mr. Dredge's house occupied by the Knights. And we come on to the Village proper; on the ground where Mr. Boorne's Brewery now stands, close to the Old Church and the entrance to the Manor House. Then opposite these, there were the shop and dwelling of Gumbrell, the *Carpenter;* of Bonwick, the *Baker;* and Cannan, the *Blacksmith*—the latter an enterprising character, who built a windmill, where is now South Beddington. It was burnt down in 1850. The earliest windmill in England was supposed to be one in our neighbourhood—at Tanrigge Priory, in the time of Richard II. (Manning.)

But we are over the hedge, into Beddington. And so we turn back to "Elm Grove"—now the property of Mr. W. F. Graham. A Mr. Potts (to whose memory is a tablet in Carshalton Church) had a house, where are now the stables and out-buildings. In the day we speak of, a Mr. Gregg occupied Elm Grove House. He was solicitor to the Skinner's Company, and agent to the Earl of Carlisle. He was celebrated for activity and strict punctuality, as a man of business. Wealthy, and going daily to London, he had a "Post-chaise" kept on purpose for him, by the master of the King's Arms Inn, Carshalton—an expensive luxury in locomotion, which many envied. He had also a large establishment of servants, in strict and admirable order; and was also noted for hospitality and luxurious dinners, which attracted not a few of the *bon-vivant caste*, to be his frequent visitors. One of these, who was most often at his table, on one occasion, did not get to Wallington as early as usual. On entering the house, he anxiously enquired of the butler whether dinner had begun; was he late? "No, sir," replied the butler, "*you* are *never* too late for *dinner!*" In the matter of punctuality, Mr Gregg was severe, and at once discharged any domestic, failing in that virtue. It is related that it was Mr. Gregg's practice to call at his banker's precisely at 9 a.m., with his cheque in his hand, to await the doors being opened; when he was the first, if not the only person, to present his cheque, impatient of a moment's delay in the clerk's giving him the cash. Verily, in our railway days, Mr. Gregg could never have been late for the train; though the train might often be late for him! But, gentle reader, "Punctuality is a virtue," not to be smiled at, so much as imitated.

Where is now the "Rose and Crown," were a lot of old tenements. We noticed the "long-room," made out of the lower rooms of two cottages, to make our first Girl's SCHOOL. Mr. West had occupied one. The beams across, though it is not apparent through the whitewash, are "Spanish chesnut" —"hard as iron." "Quality Row" has much of similar timber, which is frequently found in buildings of 200 years ago, or more. "Parkfields," where Mrs. Cox lives, was built about seventy years ago. The House where Mr. Mackenzie's resides belonged to the Fry family, who, in 1762, bought the Manor of Banstead from the Carews. The principal part of the building may date back 200 years, or more. The House which is the property of Mr. N. Bridges, was, in 1610, usually called Wallington Place; and then the

"Manor House." (The residences of the Lords of the Manor are often called "Places.") Of late years it has been called "Wallington House."

The locality where we now are should be of especial interest to our neighbours, "the Village" on the West, which, according to the most trustworthy county histories, acquired " its present name from some Cross in the neighbourhood. In Domesday it was called *Aultone*, *q. d.*, the Old Town; then Cross-Aultone, which by degrees became Cressalton, Kershalton, and so Carshalton." Aubrey quotes an old Deed of Sir Henry Burton's, by which it appeared that there was a parcel of land belonging to the Priory of Merton—partly in Carshalton and partly in Wallington— devised by Henry VIII. to the Burtons, for the yearly rent of 25s. 6d., and was granted to William Blake in the same manner, etc. These lands were called the "Crosslands," and they appear to have come into possession of Sir Baptist Hicks—a name connected with the county of Middlesex, from his munificent gift of a *Sessions House*, "Hicks' Hall." He was afterwards created Viscount Campden, with remainder, after his decease, to his son-in-law, Lord Noel (whence Earl Gainsborough). This Lord Noel's mother was a sister of our Sir James Harrington. Sir Baptist sold these Crosslands 9th of August, 1609, to Thomas Flavers, Esq. The lands immediately adjacent to our Village answer the above description; and the site of the old Cross; such being frequently met with in Villages, and at the intersection of great thoroughfares, during mediæval times. In Cheam, such a Cross stood at *Lynce's Corner*, marking the concurrence of the Parishes of Cheam, Cuddington, and Mitcham. (Brayley). The rent of

25s. 6d. would represent but a small estate, even in those days. In Edward III. arable land was 6d. per acre; growing ten bushels of wheat, worth 6d. per bushel. In 1599, a quarter of wheat was £1 7s. In 1601, a labourer had 10d. a day; a master mason, 1s. 2d. It would then take the mason three days to earn enough money to buy a bushel of wheat; now he could buy it with less than half that time's labour. In 1644, it appears, from a curious document (quoted in Manning iii., 80), the average value of land in Surrey was 8s. per acre.

But to proceed. Miss Loraine's house was built by a Mr. Wright, who also built the cottages, *Wright's Row*, on the right hand side of the road, leading up to the *Rookery*. On the left hand side we have *Oxdon's Place*, and *Whitehall*. There was, in that day, no house where Mrs. Lumb resides. Mr. Robert Loraine commenced building operations there with a large room, which now is the drawing-room. Here commenced the first Musical Society in Wallington—a band of upwards of twenty instruments; afterwards about thirty voices. Mr. Loraine and others added to the house at different periods.

We come back again to the Green. "The Bowling Green," about A.D. 1800, with lots of children at play— no School then. On the Sunday, the women in scarlet cloaks; the men in white frocks. The "Duke's Head" was then a low thatched cottage of two rooms only, with steps to go down into it. On the right hand of Manor Road were a number of small tenements, occupied by the labouring class; till Mr. Juggins came, and "Manor Terrace" arose; while, consequent on these improvements, the old *Holloway*, or *Hollow Road*, became Manor *Road* also. How changed is the prospect, now, from the Manor Terrace! Then, it was over extensive bleaching grounds. Next came "the Enclosure" and the "Field Gardens," for the "Labourer's Friend Society," with the Lavender fields and the *Physic Gardens.* To extract the virtues from the gardens' produce, Mr. Lee built a *Still.* But more picturesque eastward, we have the Almshouses (*St. Mary's Hospital*), erected in memory of the Rev. James Hamilton; and since added to, by two connections of that gentleman, offering lodgings and sundry small aids to ten poor people out of the old Parish of Beddington-cum-Wallington. The appointment, according to the original Trust Deed, is with the Rector and Churchwardens of Beddington; alternately with the Minister and Churchwardens of the New Church —at Wallington. The Building is situated in the Parish of Holy Trinity, Wallington, but the spiritual oversight was reserved for the Rector of Beddington, by his special desire, in the order of Council, December, 1867. Then we have, close to the Almshouses, Mr. Wood's residence, "The Mains," perpetuating the memory of the name usually attached to that locality, and doubtless originating in the fact that the land thereabouts (good land!) had been in earliest times reserved for the Lord of the Manor, as his peculiar "demesne"—*domain.* Then only a few years ago, it seemed as if Wallington might one day rival Battersea, to which foolish people were advised to "go to be cut for the simples." *Grose* tells us the proverb originated in the quantity of medicinal herbs grown there; which the London apothecaries, who had purchased them, were careful to have gathered at the proper season of the year; and so they went to Battersea to see their *simples* cut. It was

all open country to Woodcote Lodge, then the property of
Mr. H. Durand, now of Mr. M. Meryweather Turner.

But these are things of the past. The Railroad came—
facilities increased for reaching the metropolis without
incurring the expense of keeping a *yellow post-chaise;* and
the Freehold Land Society took a plot for building. Other
adventurous spirits commenced—Messrs. Nicholls, Crowley,
and others. Then the Church arrived; and Danbury Terrace; and Alcester Road; and Harcourt Road; call up
memories of a past—to return no more. And other roads
and Villas we cannot now mention. What was open
country only, is now gradually throwing up a crop of
houses; and the Town on *Wallington Plateau* will claim a
place in the "Historical Notes" of some future compiler.
People no longer find it *necessary* to go to "*the Village*"
(Carshalton) as of old, though its tradesmen still hold their
high character; but pause on the road occasionally, and
find it convenient and profitable to do their little shoppings
not so far from home; and with our good friends at Beddington, we almost rival Croydon High Street! What we
shall be in future, who can foreseé? "We hope indeed for
the best"—"Palmam qui meruit, ferat."

We have our attractions, we think—of Climate notably.
Situated on the borders of the Chalk District, that part of
the Hamlet of Wallington which is comprehended in the
Parish of Holy Trinity—that is to say, Wallington proper
—attains a considerable elevation. Its lowest point at
Wallington Bridge is $93\frac{1}{2}$ feet above the mean tide level.
At Wallington Church it is 141 feet; Rosemount, 197 feet;
while at Woodcote it reaches 267 feet. (Ordnance Map.)
The land to the southwards and westwards is of even

higher elevation. Woodmansterne Rectory, which seems in a deep valley, is level with the top of St. Paul's, London. It is no presumption to claim for Wallington, on the "Surrey Hills," a purer atmosphere and a more bracing air than the lower situations of the adjoining Villages can claim. Thus we can offer a suitable Sanatorium to the overworked brains of our great Metropolis. Indeed our character, in this respect, has been proved by the many who came to reside as invalids, and are now in the enjoyment of good health. It is accessible by railway in half an hour; or by road, from either Westminster or London Bridge, it is a drive of ten miles.

A striking peculiarity of freedom from Storms should be noticed. Oftentimes the thunder-clouds burst on the West and East, and South, without more than a very small portion falling in our Parish. Last summer, in the month of July, a very heavy storm flooded Croydon, and only stayed its course by Beddington. One could have counted the drops at Wallington; but the same storm fell heavily at Cheam and Ewell. In a gentleman's house at Ewell, the lightning passed along the side of one room, and brought down all the pictures from the wall.

Then what shall we say of our "blue transparent Vandalis," so tempting to the disciples of Isaac Walton? or of the excellent partridge shooting, even amongst the mint and lavender? These are privileges reserved for the favoured few, who can obtain permission from the landowners to indulge in that sport. And the packs of hounds, with frequent meets near at hand, must be put aside, if we would offer some relaxation, and an object to which "the many" may look for enjoyment. We think there is one pursuit, at least, that may be taken up, to the great benefit of health and mental instruction. For if "My Garden" has its wonders, certainly the neighbourhood of "My Garden" has its attractions, which the Wild Flora of the district may supply. If one is an enthusiast in this branch of Natural History, the railroad will take the Botanist to Banstead Village (572 feet above the level of the sea) and *Banstead Downs* in twenty minutes; or *Boxhill* may be reached in half an hour; Leith Hill, adjoining, is 967 feet, the highest elevation in the county—neighbourhoods, where are to be found the richest treasures of the County Flora. A stroll through Norbury Park and Juniper Hall grounds, will fill a vasculum with almost every variety of Orchis; while various kinds of Ferns abound. But our own immediate neighbourhood is not deficient, as may be gathered from the perusal of the following papers on the subject, contributed by two friends, as a Supplement to our "Historical Notes."

Glance at a "Note" we have, from one of our Poets, of the scenes to which we invite you:—

> .   .   .   .   .   " spacious airy downs—
> With grass and thyme o'erspread and clover wild,
> Where smiling Phœbus tempers every breeze,
> The fairest flock rejoice.
> Such as the Downs of Banstead, edged with woods
> And tow'ry villas."—
>
> DYER'S FLEECE.—Book I.

BOTANICAL WALKS ABOUT WALLINGTON.

WALK FIRST.

You want me to direct you to some Botanical treasures in the neighbourhood of my early home; so gladly will I accompany you in some of my rambles, and well assured am I that they need not be barren of objects of interest. For Wallington is a favoured spot, from the circumstance of its combining the varieties of chalk, sand, and marshy ground in the soil of its vicinity. As a proof that the Flora is by no means meagre, I may tell you, that a lady in the neighbourhood made a collection, in a few days, of no fewer than 100 British plants ; and were the collection extended over all the months of the year, many more might be added to that number.

But now, perhaps, the pleasantest way of proceeding would be to sketch out one or two walks, and to indicate some lovely, or rare, or curious plants, which you may find in each direction.

First then, suppose you start along the high road from Wallington, passing the Beddington National Schools, turning to the left to the fine old Parish Church, behind which stands the baronial Mansion of the Carew family— now occupied as a Female Orphan Asylum. You must go and see that one day, but must not stop now, except to gather from the picturesque, low, broad churchyard wall, the curious little Pellitory of the wall, *Parietaria officinalis*,

the filaments of which, as they advance to maturity, uncoil
with considerable elastic force. Diverging to the right as
soon as you have passed the Church, a fine avenue will
bring you to the high road; and it is worth the dètour,
though it lengthens the walk a little, because there, among
the little turfy hillocks of the field, on the left of the avenue,
may be found the ever welcome and duly prized sweet violet.
Many a handful have I gathered there, prized even above
their rich garden sisters, just because they were wild; and
I have a pleasant recollection, as unfading as the sweet
scent of those flowers, of a bright-eyed, shy, little village
boy, who used to meet me daily, and thrust a little nosegay
of them into my hand, and then run off almost before I
could thank him. There too, and even in the very dusty,
hard road, you may find, in the early spring, tightly curled
up into a whitish green pipe, the first leaves of the "Lords
and Ladies"—the *arum maculatum*—forcing their way with
that marvellous strength *of life* which overcomes every
impediment in the young plant's search for light. Is not
"coming to light" a sure sign of life? I need hardly re-
mind you, that this green-sheathed "lady," the great delight
of village children—though its unpleasant smell makes it
unwelcome to many—is closely allied with the Arum, from
which arrowroot is manufactured. Its root is said to possess
nutritious properties; and there is a tradition that it was
ground and boiled for food, at one season of scarcity in
England. The sand-pit bank is gay in spring with the
delicate little *Stellaria Holostia*, with its needle-leaves;
bright with the gay *Veronica chamœdrys*, the Germander
Speedwell—*not*, as sometimes called, the Forget-me-not.
Of this lovely family (for though they vary very much in

size and form, they are all very beautiful) there may be found a curious little species, growing on the garden wall, on the left hand side of the high road leading to Waddon; it has some flowerets of sulphur-colored, or yellow blossoms, all very minute, and finally changing to blue as they shrivel and fade. On the same wall, and still more abundantly on garden walls at Waddon, may be found the delicate little *Draba Verna*, rearing its fragile stem out of its star of green root leaves, and bearing its small crown of seed-pearl flowers. Turn now to the left, till you come in face of the Waddon flour mills; another little digression—this time to the right, a little way up a pretty lane—will be amply repaid, by bringing you to a fine habitat of the Butter-bur, *Pitasites vulgaris*, a very injurious weed in moist meadows; but very handsome, notwithstanding, are its early flesh-coloured flowers, growing in the form called a "thyrsus," and appearing like pinkish plumes, along the margin of the Wandle. The leaves are roundish, heart-shaped, and covered with a white down underneath; they attain an enormous size, whence the name (Petasos, *Greek*)—a covering to the head, or umbrella, and do not appear till after the flowers. This spot is famous in the neighbourhood for the abundant growth of the unrivalled large blue Forget-me-not; the very stream seems to have caught the hue of the sky, so covered is it by that lovely weed. It will please your young companions to gather a large quantity, and fastening the heads of the flowers to a slight wire ring, in the form of a wreath, lay it in a saucer of water; it will keep in fresh beauty for weeks. When satisfied with the beauties of these water, or marsh flowers (and if time permitted, much of interest might be found in the true water

plants that thrive in the running stream—the Lemnas and
the Potomagetons, with their worlds of animalculæ clothing
their leaves, and affording infinite amusement and instruction as seen under the microscope) ; but when, I say, you
can turn away from these attractions, proceed by the river's
side towards Beddington, on your return homewards.
Along the shady parts of the path you may find abundance
of the tiny pinkish-white Enchanter's Nightshade, *Circœa
Lutetiana*, which has nothing in common with the Deadly
Nightshade, *Solanum Dulcamara*, except the trivial name,
though it may be very probably growing in closer proximity
to it.

Passing over "Brandy-bottle Hill," on your right between
the path and the river, you must venture to disregard the
awful warning against trespassers, if you would find the
rare and pretty little Fern, *Botrychium Lunaria*, the common
Moonwort, one of the so-called flowering ferns, because the
fructification is on one frond, and almost covers it, while
the other frond is barren. The branched cluster of capsules
resembles a bunch of grapes, while the pinnæ of the usually
solitary barren frond are moon-shaped. Ferns are not very
abundant at Wallington, and in that neighbourhood, which
makes this singular little Fern the more to be prized. I
have seen the *Ruta-muraria*, the Wall Rue, on a high brick
wall (out of reach), and the Hart's Tongue, at Wallington;
but these are the only Ferns I remember in this locality,
with the exception, of course, of the common Brake.

Not far from the habitat of the Botrychium Lunaria, you
may come upon the pure white *Saxifraga granulata*, with
its kidney-shaped obtusely-lobed, long-stalked, radical leaves,
whilst those of the upper part of the stem are nearly sessile

H

and acutely-lobed. But the principal characteristic of the plant is the existence of numerous small clustered tubers underground, like grains, whence its name. The river Wandle is seen here at its loveliest—so sparkling, and clear and rapid. I forgot to mention, but you will scarcely omit to notice the queen of British flowers—the pure white water lily, basking in the sunshine, and supported on her broad green rafts of leaves, at the bridge, near the mill. But as you reach the end of Beddington Lane, and begin leaving it on your right, to wind round up Chat's Hill, towards the Post Office, you may observe a veritable "cloth of gold" spread by the rich broad blossoms of the Marsh Marygold, the *Caltha palustris*. It grows in the mud, and therefore defies lady admirers; but only persuade a little urchin to tuck up his trousers, and bring you a handful, and then place them in a vase of water, and your drawing-room will look gorgeous in their golden splendour. As you now hasten homewards, one modest little flower may attract your notice; it is the *Sisymbrium Irio*—Broad Hedge Mustard, with peculiar delicately-tinted yellow flowers, and long erect pods. It is said to have covered the ground after the great fire of London, 1666. You will find plenty of occupation in examining your collection; and if you intend to make a Hortus Siccus, let me advise you to place your specimens between sheets of writing paper, and not blotting paper, as this method preserves the colours much better.

J. L.

————

WALK SECOND.

Coming from the moors and uplands of Somersetshire— so rich in a brilliant and delicate flora, to the neighbour-

hood of Wallington, one is inclined to think it is entirely
barren of interesting wild plants; but a few walks, with
botany as one's object, quite undeceives one. So if you will
set forth some August evening, on what (with a very slight
digression) will be a *Wallington walk*, you will be able to
cull a bouquet, fit for any lady's drawing-room.

Starting from Wallington Green, take a few steps along
the Beddington road, an opening in the hedge discloses a
new road—Harcourt Road, bordered on the right by a row
of unfinished villas, and on the left by the grounds of a
nurseryman. "Naught here," you will say, "for my
bouquet." But stay. What see we here, spreading its
slender little branches, with its beautiful whorls of leaves,
and lovely clusters of lilac flowers, over the very stones of
the half-made road? Why, a splendid specimen of the
Field Madder, *Sherardia arvensis*. Pluck a specimen, and
pass on to the end of the villas; thence onwards, on what
some would declare to be a Roman Causeway, parallel with
the "Hollow-Way." Here, right and left, your path is gay
with the untidy-looking Chicory, or Succory—*Cichorium
intybus*, whose inelegant appearance is compensated by its
lovely blue, star-like flowers, and from the fact of their
opening at eight o'clock a.m., and closing at four p.m., the
plant has gained the appellative, "poor man's clock." It
is closely allied to the beautiful spring salad *Endive*, and the
Succory itself is largely eaten by the Egyptians. From
the root is obtained the *Chicory*, so much used to adulterate
coffee. But look, on your right, at the flaunting purple
blossoms of the Corn Cockle—*Agrostemma githago*, aptly
called the "Crown of the Field," well loved by the botanist
but not by the farmer; its black, shining seeds being specially

H 2   L. of C.

detested by him. A little further on, you come upon the curious Blue Flea-bane—*Erigeron acris*, with its clusters of flowers of yellow centres and dusky purplish rays; in a week or so, its little feathery seeds will look like branches of tawny down. Close to this you can pluck the pure white Campion—*Lychnis vespertina*, which, as it is evening, will charm you with its fragrance : hence its name. Nor must we pass these particularly-large blossoms of the Dove's-foot Crane's-bill, *Geranium molle*, tiny even here, but mark its almost circular, many-lobed leaves ; and then hasten onwards towards the Railway bridge, diverge to the left, and leaving Cathcart Road on your right, cross the open waste piece of ground. Here, in the earlier part of the year, I have found the curious Bird's-nest Orchis, *Listeria nidus-avis*, pushing its head of brown up through the chalk. Pass on to the high road to Croydon, past the Windmill Field. But stay a moment, to pluck from this weedy place on the right, a blossom of the Corn Spurrey, *Spergula arvensis*, with its strange thread-like bunches of leaves and pretty white flower.

And now we must leave the parish of Wallington, and keep the road, until we reach the new temporary Church of Bandon Hill, turn to the right, along a road, brilliant with the rich purple blossoms and tri-coloured clusters of berries of the Solanum Dulcamara, at the end we arrive at " Goose Green ;" and here we find a greater favourite, the beautiful Harebell—*Campanula Rotundifolia*—the " Blue-bell of Scotland," waving its lovely bells in the breeze. On turning sharply to the right, we re-enter Wallington, and are greeted with the gaudy yellow Goat's-beard—*Tragopogon pratensis*. Wait a week or so, and then look for its seed.

But here is one, not just like the Dandelion clocks we used to love to puff, but each white seed has a stalk of its own, round which are set its delicate little hairs, like tiny parasols, shorn of their coverings. And here, too, aspiring even to the lower branches of the sturdy oak, clasping the smoother stem of the chesnut, and twining in saucy glee with the aromatic fir-tree, we see the Traveller's Joy— *Clematis vitalba*, throwing out its long tendrils of white tufty flowers, which soon will turn to what will look like feathery down.

Our bouquet, however, will not be complete without some sprays of the Yellow Bedstraw—*Galium Verum*, whose feathery blossoms garnish it beautifully, and whose root yields a dye equal, if not superior, to *madder*, only it is too small to admit of its adaptation. Now, as we are almost close to the rose-covered station of Wallington, you may think our gatherings are at an end. But no. Almost side by side we find some splendid specimens of the Small Scabious—*Scabiosa Columbaria*, and Field Knautia— *Knautia arvensis*. Pluck some of the largest blossoms. Survey your *nosegay;* and now will you say that Wallington is barren of interesting wild plants ?

L. C. B.

WALK THIRD.

If prepared for another walk, we will start this bright August morn from Wallington, and taking our path through the village of Carshalton, past the Church, the beautiful ponds and Anne Boleyn's well, and leaving Carshalton House on our right, press onwards to the top of Park Hill.

Here we take the least frequented road on the right hand side, close to the large chalk-pit; on either side it is fringed by many specimens of the Parsley tribe. But hasten onwards to the railway arch; just mount the bank on the left side, and examine the field just cleared of corn, you will find the trailing, little branches, with the round downy leaves and lovely yellow purple-tipped blossoms of the round-leaved Fluellen—*Linaria spuria,* a diminutive plant, but most interesting, and not very common. Pass under the arch, climb the fence on the right, and scramble along the embankment of the Epsom and Dorking line. Here, half way up, you see the lovely rose-coloured blossoms of the Rose-bay Willow Herb—*Epilobium augustifolium.* The plant itself is stunted, but its blossoms are as rich in colour as those of the largest specimen. Close by, we find the square-stalked Willow Herb—*Epilobium tetragonum,* with flowers of a paler colour, and considerably smaller than its neighbour, but nevertheless peculiar, for the distinct angles of its stem, and the great length of its pod-like vessels.

Retracing our steps to the road, we pass onwards towards the Barrow-Hedges Farm, and again we must put ourselves in danger of being thought unfeminine, for in the rough piece of grazing land on the left, we spy some of the rich crimson heads of the Saint Foin—*Onobrychis sativa,* which, though sometimes cultivated, nevertheless may be numbered among our wild plants. Returning to the road, we find, on our right, the Fumitory—*Fumaria officinalis,* with the rich purplish crimson flowers, and delicate, much divided leaves.

But pass onwards, the road on either side being a perfect galaxy of beauties, and the air perfumed with the scents of the Wild Thyme and Marjoram; but the dense, yellow heads of the sulphur-coloured Trefoil—*Trifolium ochroleu-crum*, will be sure to attract special notice; and also the fine blossoms of its near neighbour, the Bird's-foot Trefoil— *Lotus Corniculatus*—"the shoes and stockings" of child-hood's days; while, at our feet, find the Rest Harrow— *Ononis arvensis*, with its rose-coloured pea-shaped blossoms. But search the bank more closely, and you see the sweet little blossoms of the Eyebright—*Euphrasia officinalis*. Here it is rather small, but on the Epsom Downs it is par-ticularly large and plentiful. Its often neighbour, the Cathartic Flax—*Linum catharticum*, and here also we find it;—has blossoms of the purest white, and like little vases in shape, but very tiny, the whole plant being scarcely six inches in height. We have now reached the back of Barrow-Hedges (so named from the ancient "barrows," mentioned by antiquaries as being on this rising ground), and if you are not inclined to trespass and make a path at right angles with your present road across the fields to Woodcote, you must retrace your steps as far as the farm, as no other road presents itself, turning sharply to the right, climb the rising ground till you reach the Beech Tree Walk. Leave this road, and pursue your way past a group of new houses, and sinking into the hollow, turn abruptly to the right, along side of the Woodcote grounds, generally supposed to have been the site of a British or Roman city. An unfrequented road, bordering the wood, gives us many floral treasures, already mentioned; and, in addition, we find the Perforated St. John's Wort—*Hypericum perforatum*; the Common Purple Trefoil—*Trifolium pra-tense;* and the Discoid Knapweed—*Centaurea nigra*. This path will bring us as far as Mr. Arnott's farm, whence we can return to Wallington by the high road.   L. C. B.

"THE BEST COLLECTION OF WILD FLOWERS (93)
FOUND IN THE MONTH OF AUGUST, 1872, IN THE
NEIGHBOURHOOD OF WALLINGTON;"

For which was awarded, as a prize, a copy of "My Garden," by
A. SMEE, Esq., on the auspicious occasion of the Marriage of his
daughter, 20th August, 1872.

1.	*Senecio Jacobea*	Common Yellow Ragwort.
2.	,, *Vulgaris*	Common Groundsel.
3.	*Achillœa millefolium*	Yarrow.
4.	*Urtica dioica*	Stinging Nettle.
5.	*Lamium album*	White dead Nettle.
6.	,, *purpureum*	Red dead Nettle.
7.	*Galeopsis Tetrahit*	Common Hemp Nettle.
8.	*Euphorbia Helioscopia*	Sun Spurge.
9.	,, *Exigua*	Dwarf Spurge.
10.	*Reseda Luteola*	Rocket.
11.	*Solanum Dulcamara*	Woody Nightshade.
12.	,, *Nigrum*	Common Nightshade.
13.	*Campanula Rotundifolia*	Harebell.
14.	*Agrostemma Githago*	Corn Cockle.
15.	*Papaver Rhœas*	Red Poppy.
16.	*Anagallis arvensis*	Red Pimpernel.
17.	*Convolvulus arvensis*	Small Convolvulus.
18.	,, *Sepium*	Major Convolvulus.
19.	*Thymus Serpyllnm*	Wild Thyme.
20.	*Origanum vulgare*	Marjoram.
21.	*Bartsia Odontitus*	Red Bartsia.
22.	*Linaria vulgaris*	Yellow Toad-flax.
23.	,, ˉ*spuria*	Round-leaved Fluellen.
24.	*Eupatoria agrimonia*	Agrimony.

25. *Hieracium Umbellatum*	Hawkweed.
26. *Antirrhinum*	Snapdragon.
27. *Artemisia vulgaris*	Wormwood.
28. *Silene inflata*	Bladder Campion.
29. *Arenaria serpyllifolia*	Thyme-leaved Sandwort.
30. „ *tenufolia*	Fine-leaved Sandwort.
31. *Rubus Fructicosus*	Bramble.
32. *Potentilla Reptans*	Creeping Cinquefoil.
33. *Potentilla Anserina*	Silverweed.
34. *Lotus Corinculatus*	Bird's-foot Trefoil.
35. *Trifolium ochroleucum*	Sulphur-coloured Trefoil.
36. „ *repens*	Dutch Clover.
37. *Cichorum Intybus*	Succory.
38. *Geum urbanum*	Herb Bennet.
39. *Malva Sylvestris*	Common Mallow.
40. „ *rotundifolia*	Dwarf Mallow.
41. *Sinapis arvensis*	Charlock.
42. *Salvia Verbenacea*	Wild Sage.
43. *Knautia arvensis*	Field Knautia.
44. *Galium Verum*	Yellow Bedstraw.
45. „ *Mollugo*	Great Hedge Bedstraw.
46. „ *Aparine*	Cleavers.
47. *Sherardia arvenis*	Blue Field Madder.
48. *Epilobium augustifolium*	Rose-bay Willow Herb.
49. „ *tetragonum*	Square-stalked Willow Herb.
50. *Anthemis nobilis*	Camomile.
51. *Verbena officinalis*	Vervain.
52. *Clematis Vitalba*	Traveller's Joy.
53. *Tragopogon pratensis*	Yellow Goat's-beard.
54. *Thalspi-bursa pastoris*	Shepherd's Purse.
55. *Potentilla Tormentilla*	Tormentil.

56. *Ulex Europæus*	Furze.
57. *Geranium Robertianum*	Herb Robert.
58. „ *molle*	Dove's-foot Crane's-bill.
59. „ *pyrenaicum*	Mountain Crane's-bill.
60. *Hypericum pulchrum*	St. John's Wort.
61. *Onobrychis Sativa*	Saint Foin.
62. *Bellis perennis*	Daisy.
63. *Arctium Lappa*	Burdock.
64. *Erica vulgaris*	Common Ling.
65. „ *cineria*	Fine-leaved Heath.
66. *Solidago virgaurea*	Common Golden Rod.
67. *Centaurea Jacca*	Brown-rayed Knapweed.
68. „ *nigra*	Discoid Knapweed.
69. *Illicebrum verticillatum*	Whorled Knot Grass.
70. *Runex*	Dock.
71. *Chrysanthemnm Leucanthemum*	Great White Ox eye.
72. *Ranunculus Hirsatus*	Pale Buttercup.
73. *Barbarea vulgaris*	Bitter Cress.
74. *Sisymbrium officinale*	Common Hedge Mustard.
75. *Cincus Palustris*	Marsh Thistle.
76. „ *acanthoides*	Welted Thistle.
77. *Tanacetum vulgare*	Common Tansy.
78. *Erigeron acris*	Blue Flea-bane.
79. *Pulicaria Dysenteria*	Common Flea-bane.
80. *Ononis arvensis*	Common Rest Harrow.
81. *Ligusticum-scoticum*	Lovage.
82. *Fumaria officinalis*	Common Fumitory.
83. *Myosotis palustris*	Forget-me-not.
84. „ *arvensis*	Common Field Scorpion Grass
85. *Erythræa Centaurium*	Centaury.
86. *Leontodon Taraxacum.*	Common Dandelion.

87.	*Polygonum Persicaria*	Spotted Persicaria.
88.	*Stachys Sylvestris*	Wound Wort.
89.	*Vicia cracca*	Tufted Vetch.
90.	*Chenepodium Bonus Henricus*	Goosefoot.
91.	*Lapsana communis*	Nipple Wort.
92.	*Sonchus oleraceus*	Common Sow Thistle.
93.	*Trifolium medium*	Zigzag Trefoil.

THE FOLLOWING ALSO ARE FOUND IN
THE NEIGHBOURHOOD.

1.	*Euphrasia officinalis*	Eyebright.
2.	*Viola Tricolor*	Heartease.
3.	*Spergula arvensis*	Corn Spurrey.
4.	*Nasturtium officinale*	Watercress.
5.	*Veronica Beccabunga*	Brooklime.
6.	*Lythrum Salicara*	Spiked Purple Loose Strife.
7.	*Helianthemum Vulgare*	Common Rock Rose.
8.	*Polygonum Lapathifolium*	Pale-coloured Persicaria
9.	*Fœniculum vulgare*	Fennel.
10.	*Linaria Cymbalaria*	Ivy-leaved Toad-flax.
11.	*Chelidonium majus*	Common celandine.
12.	*Lychnis vespertina*	White Campion.
13.	*Hieracium umbellatum*	Narrow-leaved Hawkweed.
14.	*Scabiosa Columbaria*	Small Scabious
15.	*Linum Cartharticum*	Cathartic Flax.
16.	*Veronica serpyllifolia*	Thyme-leaved Speedwell.
17.	*Sisymbrium Irio*	(London Rocket) Broad Hedge Mustard.

18. *Echium vulgare*   Common Viper's Bugloss
19. *Scrophularia Aquatica*   Water Figwort.
20. *Plantago Lanceolata*   Ribwort Plantain.
21. *Hyacinthus-non-scriptus*   Blue-bell.
22. *Iris Pseud-acorus*   Yellow Iris.
23. *Polygonum convolvulus*   Climbing Persicaria.
24. *Tussilago Farfara*   Colt's-foot.
25. *Anthemis Cotula*   Stinking Camomile.
26. *Vinca minor*   Lesser Periwinkle.
27. *Byronia Dioica*   White Bryony.
28. *Prunus Spinosa*   Sloe.
29. *Dipsacus sylvestris*   Wild Teazel.
30. *Primula veris*   Cowslip.
31. *Cerastium viscosum*   Viscid Mouse-ear Chickweed.

L. C. B.

APPENDIX

TO

HISTORICAL NOTES.

APPENDIX A.

We are enabled to supply some highly interesting "Notes" on the site of Nœomagus, by C. W. Standidge, Esq., referring to the statements of ancient authors.

He, first of all, takes the figures from Horsley's "Brittannia Romana" (A.D. 1732), a book of very high repute; in which the English portion of Ptolemy's Geography is translated. Ptolemy gives

London as in long. 20 deg. 00 min. W., and lat. 53 deg. 00 min. N.

Nœomagus ,, 19 ,, 45 ,, W., ,, 53 ,, 25 ,, N.

Venta ,, 18 ,, 40˙ ,, W., ,, 53 ,, 30 ,, N.

Without entering into the somewhat difficult question of the methods by which Ptolemy computed his latitude and longitude, we may fairly assume his degree of longitude was 35 to 40 miles; and his degree of latitude about 60, in the present case. Then

I. VENTA (which is unquestionably WINCHESTER) and Nœomagus, lie, west of London, in the proportion of 1' 20" to 15", i.e., of 80—15. Winchester is 53 miles west of London—then Nœomagus is 15-80ths. of 53 miles; or very nearly 10 miles.

II. Venta is 30" south of London, and Nœomagus 25"—then these two places would lie south of London in the proportion of 30—25. Winchester is 31 miles south of London—then Nœomagus is 25-30ths. of 31 miles south of London. To place Nœomagus, according to Ptolemy's view, we must find some place which lies 10 miles W. and 25m. 5-6ths. S. of London—meaning, of course, the centre of the old Roman city, which we should fix about Watling Street. And the only place answering to this description is a spot between Capel, in Surrey, and Rusher, in Sussex. Now, this point just hits off the STANE STREET (p. 6), and the locality of ANSTIEBURY Camp exactly answers.

Again. Ptolemy makes Nœomagus the chief town of the "Regni." the people of Surrey and Sussex, "to the south of the Atrebatii and Cantii"—the former people extending from Berkshire, S. of the Thames, till they touched the W. border of the Cantii (Kent). If Nœomagus was at Woodcote, the Regni must have had their principal town in a bad position for defence; which is possible, though not likely. As far as Ptolemy is concerned, his Nœomagus certainly points to ANSTIEBURY. But in all probability he was never in Britain; and so his information, obtained through others, as to the astronomical position of places, in themselves very obscure, may not be perfectly reliable.

Therefore Mr. Standidge gives "much greater value to the more practical figures contained in 'Itinerary of Antoninus.'" (p 4.) He then lays down as a "universally admitted fact," that "Durobrivis" is Rochester. The distance thence to London, by Coach-road, was, in Horsley's time, 29¾ miles, measured probably from the Standard, in Cornhill, from whence the old mile stones, S. of London, were generally reckoned (the spot would be nearly opposite the shop of Messrs. Silver); and this Coach road would probably have followed the old Roman road, in a great measure. Dr. W. Smith, in his Dictionary of Greek and Roman Antiquities, gives two independent calculations of the Roman mile, which result, one 1,614 and the other in 1,618 yards, as its length. Taking 1,616 yards, as the mean of the two reckonings, we find that the distance from London to Rochester, by the "Antonine route," to be 37 "Roman" miles, and this distance is just under 34 English statute miles of 1,760 yards each. Now, the distance from Wallington to Rochester, as the crow would fly, is at least 28 statute miles; while that from Wallington to the nearest part of Roman London (say Queenhithe) exceeds 10 miles. If, therefore, Noviomagus be at Wallington, we must suppose that a distance, which when measured on the map is from 38 to 40 miles, would be traversed by road in 34 miles, the crossing of the Thames being, perhaps, included in the reckoning.

The difficulty is still further increased, if we agree with the majority of critics, that "Vagniacis" is Northfleet, which lies three or four miles to the north of the straight line between Wallington and Rochester. It is only necessary to look at a good map, and see how utterly improbable it is that a practical race like the Romans would take the route to

Rochester by Wallington. It is indeed probable that there were marshes on the S. of the Thames, impassable in winter, that would make it necessary to push back the road to avoid them. But if this were done to the line of Blackheath and Eltham, there would only be the small stream of the Ravensbourne to bridge over—a very small matter to a people who had bridged the Rhine and the Danube. And even if they kept to the firm ground, they need go no further out of their way than just to the south of the source of the Ravensbourne, altogether a distance somewhere under 31 miles in a straight line—equivalent to 34 miles of Roman road.

On the basis of the Itinerary of Antoninus, it is probable that Noviomagus is to be found at HOLWOOD HILL, in the parish of Keston, near Bromley, Kent, where are remains of a Roman Camp. This view is somewhat strengthened by Richard of Cirencester, the mediæval authority on early British topography—who wrote A.D. 1350-1400—but who evidently had access to old materials. He gives the route from Anderida (Pevensey) to London, as passing through Noviomago, which points decidedly to Holwood Hill, and his road from Chichester to London is by Winchester and Staines ; a fact which seems to suggest that the "Stane Street" was constructed in the later days of the Roman occupation of Britain.

Mr. Standidge adds, that he is inclined to believe that Woodcote was on, or close to, the Stane Street, which was probably (?) constructed after the date of the Itinerary (Antonine), but before the withdrawal of the Romans from Britain, early in the fifth century. Woodcote is in the right line and about the right distance from London for the first stage out. It was probably not a military station—partly because it is a weak position ; and partly because of the later date of the Stane Street, when a fortified camp would be unnecessary, the country being quite peaceful. What one would expect to find in such a situation would be the remains of Roman Villas, and Roadways, and Coins, mostly dating from Caracalla downwards.

Thus Mr. Standidge had written—previous to any knowledge that a Roman Villa had been discovered ; and many Roman Coins also ; in our neighbourhood. And so we will add a few remarks on these traces of Roman occupation.

APPENDIX B.

First—the COINS. We have only one of earlier date than Caracalla —that found in the field adjoining the Roman Villa—a coin of COMMODUS, Emperor from A.D. 176 to 192. It was a troublous time in Britain—with the warlike tribes of Picts and Scots in the North, and a mutinous spirit among the Roman troops. It was shortly after the death of Commodus that the Prætorian bands put up the Empire for sale to the highest bidder. Then the Roman army in Britain elected Severus Emperor. He took a very active interest in the affairs of Britain. The wall of Severus is one evidence of this. He died at York, A.D. 211, and his son Caracalla succeeded him ; but he soon left for Rome. One effect of Caracalla's administration has been mentioned in his giving the rights of Roman citizenship to all the provinces of the Empire. Then we have in our Village Museum a coin of GALLIENUS (A.D. 263), on which is clearly distinguished the ancient silvering of the brass, when the coinage was debased. He fell before the walls of Milan, and by his dying wish, CLAUDIAN was raised to the throne. A coin of his was found near the Villa. During this period there sprung up pretenders to the throne, in every province—they have been termed the "thirty tyrants." We have a coin of one, POSTHUMUS, struck in Gaul. Another coin tells of AURELIAN, A.D. 270. He recovered Britain from Tetricus, another of the thirty. Probus (p. 9) displayed much activity in settling the affairs of the northern provinces of the Empire ; and recruiting the army, largely among the German nations, settled foreign colonists in various parts. He perished in a mutiny of his troops. Diocletian became Emperor in 284. His reign was noted for a violent persecution (the tenth) of the Christians throughout the Empire. Aurelian had been arrested in the same career, while in the act of signing an edict against the Christians, by a thunderbolt falling at his feet. Alban, the first British martyr, suffered 22nd June, A.D. 286. This was the period of CARAUSIUS and ALLECTUS (p. 11), of whom coins were found at the Villa. The Roman Commander in Britain was Constantius Chlorus, father of CONSTANTINE THE GREAT. Of this Emperor we have three coins found hereabouts. A coin of CONSTANS,

I

his son, was also found near the Villa. And in our Museum is a coin of
his nephew, DELMASIUS. Then we have a coin of JULIAN, a great
nephew, who apostatized from the Christian religion. His attempt to
rebuild Jerusalem, hoping so to prove the fallacy of the prophetical
Scriptures, is well known ; and the horrible balls of fire breaking out
near the foundations and " rendering the place inacessible to the workmen, who were scorched and blasted if they approached." In his reign,
the Picts and Scots, breaking through the wall of Severus, killed a
Roman general and the Count of the Saxon Shore ; while in the reign
of Valentinian (A.D. 367) they pillaged London, and carried off many of
its inhabitants as slaves. The coin we have of VALENTINIAN is
interesting. It displays on its reverse ; not as of old, the Roman soldier
with a trophy in one hand, and in the other, a standard, the superscription
being, " Victus exercitu Romanorum "—conquered by the army of the
Romans; but the soldier here, with the Labarum (p. 68) in one hand, is
with the other raising a suppliant, and the superscription is " Gloria
Romanorum "—the glory of the Romans. One more Roman coin we
have, of GRATIAN. He had an opposing claimant in the Briton,
Maximus, whose ambition carried off in his army, to Gaul, a multitude
of the British youth, who either fell in battle, or from other causes never
returned home. Maximus was conquered by Theodosius, the last who
ruled over the whole Roman Empire, and died at Milan, A.D. 395.

As to any deficiency of coins of an earlier date than those above
mentioned ? we may state that " these are of the type usually found in
England." (As Mr. Poole writes.)

But still, are we expected to answer the question, " Where was
NŒOMAGUS, or Noviomagus ? We answer then, that we are of opinion,
with the majority, that it was AT OR NEAR TO WALLINGTON.
Ptolemy's latitude and longitude it is difficult to accommodate. But we
may note that Anstiebury and Wallington are not so far apart from each
other ON THE ROAD from the south to London ; but that we may infer
the information of Ptolemy, being incorrect, has given us by mistake
that of the ROMAN Camp instead of the BRITISH City. Then turning
to the Antonine Itinerary, we have to observe that Wallington Green is
only 10 English statute miles from London Bridge. If we take Richard
of Cirencester's XV Roman miles from the *centre* of old Roman London ;

that reckoning would land us just at WOODCOTE (p. 10). And then as to the distance from Woodcote to Rochester, if it be 28 English miles, and the total distance from London, by Noviomagus, to Rochester, was 37 Roman miles, we have only the difference between what would be the difference of "hearsay," (on which the Antonine Itinerary is mainly founded! as well as Ptolemy's account), and "positive" evidence. It is quite clear Noviomagus was considered out of the direct route. Manning makes a curious suggestion, that HOLWOOD HILL was the WOOD IN KENT, described in Domesday (p. 14). We are not willing that a ROMAN Camp should be NECESSARILY the site of a BRITISH City. But we fall back on the evidences of Roman occupation hereabouts, and ask how came this site to be so occupied? and the answer may fairly be, It was so, after the transference of the Capital of the Regni under Cogidumus, to Chichester, ON ACCOUNT OF ITS PREVIOUS BRITISH OCCUPATION. But to reconcile the differences of position and distances given, and to correct the Texts and force agreement, is beyond the ability of our "Notes." We can only, at the worst, consider ourselves in the same category as Holms Dale, partly in Surrey and partly in Kent—the scene of many indecisive contests between Saxon and Dane; of which the proverb ran—

"The vale of Holms Dale
Was never won, ne never shall."

APPENDIX C.

THE ROMAN BUILDING DISCOVERED APRIL, 1871.

A farm of about 170 acres, part of the Park Farm, at Beddington, is irrigated by the sewage of Croydon. To extend the system of irrigation there, it was necessary to have some additional trenches cut for dispersing the sewage water; and thus were brought to view some remains of " walls, undoubtedly part of a Roman building." (We quote from Mr. E. P. Loftus Brock's Paper, read at a Meeting of the British Archæological Association, by whose courtesy we are allowed to copy his plan of the building.)

"The large chamber ("1st chamber") is 16 feet 5 inches long by 9 feet 11 inches. On the Northern side of this chamber and close to the West end, there is a semi-circular apse, leading from it, by an opening 4 feet 4 inches wide carried down to the foundations. While the larger chamber is paved with flat tiles, many of which remain, yet the flooring of the apse has been at a higher level, and carried by a series of small piers formed of the same square tiles, and as if a "hypocaust," or at least a receptacle for hot air, had been beneath; but no entrance remained. Hot air might have been brought into it from elsewhere by the flue tiles (of which many were found), but none of the fragments met with were *in situ*. The walling here, although beneath the level of the paving, was plastered internally, down to the foundations."

A "2nd chamber" was discovered, eastward of the larger one, on the Northern side. This is 7 feet 9 inches by 3 feet. No sign of entrance was visible, owing, doubtless, to the inconsiderable remaining height of the walls; but the floor here also had been carried, on brick piers, to the higher level; constructed, evidently, for a hypocaust—the usual addition to the comforts of a Roman Villa.

Eastward, and quite apart from the others, a separate detached building was uncovered. This measures 11 feet by 6 feet 6 inches within the walls, and is paved with flat tiles, bedded on the well-known Roman concrete of hard mortar, formed with pounded red brick. No appearance of a doorway was found.

Westward, from the first, large chamber, a small passage, 5 ft. 3 in. by 4 ft. 9 in., paved with tiles, was met with. There were paving tiles, appearing as though calcined. Mr. Addy suggests here was the fire of the hypocaust. This passage opened into a chamber (chamber 3rd") 7 ft. 6 in. by 6 ft., having two recesses. At the angle of the first of these, and at about 1 ft. above the paving, a projecting rebate was formed in the wall by thick ribbed tiles to form a ledge, as if to receive the edge of the paving at the higher level, as before. We have thus four recesses on the North sides of the larger chambers, the paving of which must have been at a higher level, and with spaces beneath.

The foundations also showed a fourth small chamber westward, 8ft. by 3 ft., but with no sign of entrance. It may be concluded, therefore, that the pavement here was of a higher level, and approached, by a step or two, from that of the larger apartment.

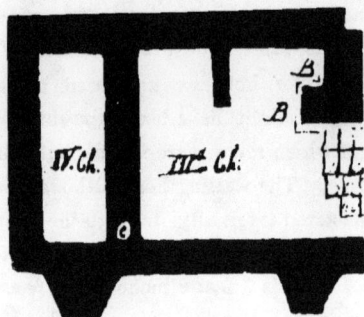

A. Brick piers
B. Ledge to receive pavemen
C. Holes cut thro' by Worker
D. Also cut thro', but an open
is supposed to have been.

L. C. B. del

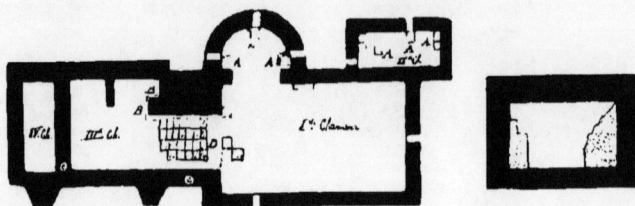

Plan of
Roman Building. discov? Feb. 1871.
on the Croydon Sewage Farm. at Beddington.

A. Brick piers
B. Ledge to receive pavement.
C. Holes cut thro' by Workmen
D. Also cut thro', but an opening
   is supposed to have been there.

L.C.B. del.

Scale: 1/10 inch to a Foot

E. P. L. B. designi

Two projecting masses on the South side may warrant the supposition that other apartments extended in this direction.

Several fragments of hard plastering were met with, having broad bands of dull red on a white ground, and remarkably fresh in colour. Many fragments of pottery also were discovered, mostly of very coarse ware; minute pieces of thin black ware, with small dots of a lighter colour; and two fragments of Samian ware. One of these has a pattern indented from an ordinary cockle-shell, impressed when the clay was wet, and alternating with what appears to be the potter's monogram. No fragments of tesselated pavement were met with. The flooring is of common red tiles, about 9 inches square, laid in mortar.

Shortly after the discovery of the site of this building, a piece of Roman brick was noticed about a furlong to the S.E.; and some excavation revealed the existence of a hard, concreted platform, about 20 feet square, and about a foot in thickness. This was composed entirely of large bricks, four inches thick, and pieces of coarse earthenware, of one inch in thickness, being portions of circular vessels of large size. No foundations of walls were met with. Had any such existed, they have been completely removed. (Could it have been a small "threshing-floor," as seen in Italy at present day? Or, since Mr. Addy mentions many fragments of large vessels or "amphoræ" found here, would these betoken a wine-press site? for many vines were grown in Britain.)

The appearance of the remains warrants the supposition that the superstructures were taken down for the sake of the building materials, since but very few fallen fragments have been found. An urn, of a very rough description, was found in another part of the field; and a considerable number of bones have been found in various directions. Other urns were met with—one of a thin black ware, with lighter stripings. A fine large circular cinerary urn was found in the field adjoining; and another less perfect urn—possibly these are Anglo-Saxon?—exhibited by Mr. Brock before the British Archæological Association.

The position of these remains affords another example of Roman buildings often erected in what are now considered most unpromising sites. The land is so low that is difficult to understand why this somewhat marshy position was selected for building, rather than the rising ground South of Beddington Church.

The walls have a remaining height of only about 18 inches from the level of the paving, while the ground level is about three feet above the paving. They are about 15 inches thick, average; and are composed of flint rubble, with a plentiful admixture of the usual flat Roman bricks, and are plastered internally and externally. The site is about the third of a mile from Beddington Church, and almost exactly North-east.

To this we may add that the sixth Vol. of the Surrey Archæological Society gives a paper by Mr. Flower, on an Anglo-Saxon Cemetery in the same field with the Villa—"about 500 yards in a southerly direction." Several skeletons and sepulchral urns were found—one of them with markings much resembling those found on some British urns. It is presumed, from the urns filled with *burnt bones*, that this cemetery was commenced in pre-Christian times, and continued in use afterwards, as the *skeletons* would suggest. Spears and daggers were found in the graves, and the iron umbo of a shield, of the usual Anglo-Saxon form.

We should add that recent alterations, at Wallington "Manor House," have brought to light various stones, built into the walls of the more recent Mansion, confirming, by the style of carving on them, the date suggested (p. 58) as that of the Mansion to which the old *Vault* belonged. One stone has the chamfers and cusping of a Gothic square-headed window; and others have the foliage which characterises the *Norman* or very *Early English* style. These relics, with portions of Roman bricks, suggest antiquarian researches in our Parish.

March, 1873.

E. L. Corker, Printer, Whitgift Street, Croydon.

www.ingramcontent.com/pod-product-compliance
Lightning Source LLC
Chambersburg PA
CBHW030608270326
41927CB00007B/1097